by Susan Sontag

AIDS and
Its Metaphors

AIDS and Its Metaphors

SUSAN SONTAG

Farrar, Straus and Giroux

NEW YORK

Copyright © 1988, 1989 by Susan Sontag

Printed in the United States of America

Published simultaneously in Canada
by Collins Publishers, Toronto

Designed by Dorris Huth

Second printing, 1989

Library of Congress Cataloging-in-Publication Data
Sontag, Susan.
AIDS and its metaphors.
1. AIDS (Disease)—Social aspects. 2. Metaphor.
I. Title.
RA644.A25S66   1988   362.1′9697′92   88–21173

Quotations from Karel Čapek's *The White Plague* are
from the translation by Michael Henry Heim, published
in *Cross Currents* 7 (1988)

———————

for Paul
August 10, 1988

AIDS and
Its Metaphors

Rereading *Illness as Metaphor* now, I thought:

1

By metaphor I meant nothing more or less than the earliest and most succinct definition I know, which is Aristotle's, in his *Poetics* (1457b). "Metaphor," Aristotle wrote, "consists in giving the thing a name that belongs to something else." Saying a thing is or is like something-it-is-not is a mental operation as old as philosophy and poetry, and the spawning ground of most kinds of understanding, including scientific understanding, and expressiveness. (To acknowledge which I prefaced the polemic against metaphors of illness I wrote ten years ago with a brief, hectic flourish of metaphor, in mock exorcism of the seductiveness of metaphorical thinking.) Of course, one cannot think without metaphors. But that does not mean there aren't some metaphors we might well abstain from or try to retire. As, of course, all thinking is interpretation. But that does not mean it isn't sometimes correct to be "against" interpretation.

Take, for instance, a tenacious metaphor that has shaped (and obscured the understanding of) so much of the political life of this century, the one that distributes, and polarizes, attitudes and social movements according to their relation to a "left" and a "right." The terms are usually traced back to the French Revolution, to the seating arrangements of the National Assembly in 1789, when republicans and radicals sat to the presiding officer's left and monarchists and conservatives sat to the right. But historical memory alone can't account for the startling longevity of this metaphor. It seems more likely that its persistence in discourse about politics to this day comes from a felt aptness to the modern, secular imagination of metaphors drawn from the body's orientation in space —left and right, top and bottom, forward and backward—for describing social conflict, a metaphoric practice that did add something new to the perennial description of society as a kind of body, a well-disciplined body ruled by a "head." This has been the dominant metaphor for the polity since Plato and Aristotle, perhaps because of its usefulness in justifying repression. Even more than comparing society to a family, comparing it to a body makes an authoritarian ordering of society seem inevitable, immutable.

Rudolf Virchow, the founder of cellular pathology, furnishes one of the rare scientifically significant examples of the reverse procedure, using political metaphors to talk about the body. In the biological controversies of the 1850s, it was the metaphor of the liberal state that Virchow found useful in advancing his theory of the cell as the fundamental unit of life. However complex their structures, organisms are, first of all, simply "multicellular"—multicitizened, as it were; the body is a "republic" or "unified common-wealth." Among scientist-rhetoricians Virchow was a maverick, not least because of the politics of his meta-phors, which, by mid-nineteenth-century standards, are antiauthoritarian. But likening the body to a society, liberal or not, is less common than comparisons to other complex, integrated systems, such as a machine or an economic enterprise.

At the beginning of Western medicine, in Greece, important metaphors for the unity of the body were adapted from the arts. One such metaphor, harmony, was singled out for scorn several centuries later by Lucretius, who argued that it could not do justice to the fact that the body consists of essential and unes-sential organs, or even to the body's materiality: that is, to death. Here are the closing lines of Lucretius' dismissal of the musical metaphor—the earliest attack I know on metaphoric thinking about illness and health:

> Not all the organs, you must realize,
> Are equally important nor does health
> Depend on all alike, but there are some—
> The seeds of breathing, warm vitality—
> Whereby we are kept alive; when these are gone
> Life leaves our dying members. So, since mind

And spirit are by nature part of man,
Let the musicians keep that term brought down
To them from lofty Helicon—or maybe
They found it somewhere else, made it apply
To something hitherto nameless in their craft—
I speak of *harmony*. Whatever it is,
Give it back to the musicians.

—*De Rerum Natura*, III, 124–35
trans. Rolfe Humphries

A history of metaphoric thinking about the body on this potent level of generality would include many images drawn from other arts and technology, notably architecture. Some metaphors are anti-explanatory, like the sermonizing, and poetic, notion enunciated by Saint Paul of the body as a temple. Some have considerable scientific resonance, such as the notion of the body as a factory, an image of the body's functioning under the sign of health, and of the body as a fortress, an image of the body that features catastrophe.

The fortress image has a long prescientific genealogy, with illness itself a metaphor for mortality, for human frailty and vulnerability. John Donne in his great cycle of prose arias on illness, *Devotions upon Emergent Occasions* (1627), written when he thought he was dying, describes illness as an enemy that invades, that lays siege to the body-fortress:

We study Health, and we deliberate upon our meats, and drink, and ayre, and exercises, and we hew and wee polish every stone, that goes to that building; and so our Health is a long and a regular work; But in a minute a Canon batters all, overthrowes all, demolishes all; a Sicknes unprevented for all our diligence, unsuspected for all our curiositie. . . .

Some parts are more fragile than others: Donne speaks of the brain and the liver being able to endure the siege of an "unnatural" or "rebellious" fever that "will blow up the heart, like a mine, in a minute." In Donne's images, it is the illness that invades. Modern medical thinking could be said to begin when the gross military metaphor becomes specific, which can only happen with the advent of a new kind of scrutiny, represented in Virchow's cellular pathology, and a more precise understanding that illnesses were caused by specific, identifiable, visible (with the aid of a microscope) organisms. It was when the invader was seen not as the illness but as the microorganism that causes the illness that medicine really began to be effective, and the military metaphors took on new credibility and precision. Since then, military metaphors have more and more come to infuse all aspects of the description of the medical situation. Disease is seen as an invasion of alien organisms, to which the body responds by its own military operations, such as the mobilizing of immunological "defenses," and medicine is "aggressive," as in the language of most chemotherapies.

The grosser metaphor survives in public health education, where disease is regularly described as invading the society, and efforts to reduce mortality from a given disease are called a fight, a struggle, a war. Military metaphors became prominent early in the century, in campaigns mounted during World War I to educate people about syphilis, and after the war about tuberculosis. One example, from the campaign against tuberculosis conducted in Italy in the 1920s, is a poster called "*Guerre alle Mosche*" (War against Flies), which illustrates the lethal effects of fly-borne diseases. The flies themselves are shown as enemy aircraft dropping bombs of death on an innocent population. The bombs have inscriptions. One says "*Microbi*," microbes. Another says "*Germi della tisi*," the germs of tuberculosis. Another simply says "*Malattia*," illness. A skeleton clad in a hooded black cloak rides the foremost fly as passenger or pilot. In another poster, "With These Weapons We Will Conquer Tuberculosis," the figure of death is shown pinned to the wall by drawn swords, each of which bears an inscription that names a measure for combating tuberculosis. "Cleanliness" is written on one blade. "Sun" on another. "Air." "Rest." "Proper food." "Hygiene." (Of course, none of these weapons was of any significance. What conquers—that is, cures—tuberculosis is antibiotics, which were not discovered until some twenty years later, in the 1940s.)

Where once it was the physician who waged *bellum contra morbum*, the war against disease, now it's the whole society. Indeed, the transformation of war-making into an occasion for mass ideological mobilization has made the notion of war useful as a metaphor for all sorts of ameliorative campaigns whose goals are cast as the defeat of an "enemy." We have had wars against poverty, now replaced by "the war on drugs," as well as wars against specific diseases, such as cancer. Abuse of the military metaphor may be inevitable in a capitalist society, a society that increasingly restricts the scope and credibility of appeals to ethical principle, in which it is thought foolish not to subject one's actions to the calculus of self-interest and profitability. War-making is one of the few activities that people are not supposed to view "realistically"; that is, with an eye to expense and practical outcome. In all-out war, expenditure is all-out, unprudent—war being defined as an emergency in which no sacrifice is excessive. But the wars against diseases are not just calls for more zeal, and more money to be spent on research. The metaphor implements the way particularly dreaded diseases are envisaged as an alien "other," as enemies are in modern war; and the move from the demonization of the illness to the attribution of fault to the patient is an inevitable one, no matter if patients are thought of as victims. Victims suggest innocence. And innocence, by the inexorable logic that governs all relational terms, suggests guilt.

•

Military metaphors contribute to the stigmatizing of certain illnesses and, by extension, of those who are ill. It was the discovery of the stigmatization of people who have cancer that led me to write *Illness as Metaphor*.

Twelve years ago, when I became a cancer patient, what particularly enraged me—and distracted me from my own terror and despair at my doctors' gloomy prognosis—was seeing how much the very reputation of this illness added to the suffering of those who have it. Many fellow patients with whom I talked during my initial hospitalizations, like others I was to meet during the subsequent two and a half years that I received chemotherapy as an outpatient in several hospitals here and in France, evinced disgust at their disease and a kind of shame. They seemed to be in the grip of fantasies about their illness by which I was quite unseduced. And it occurred to me that some of these notions were the converse of now thoroughly discredited beliefs about tuberculosis. As tuberculosis had been often regarded sentimentally, as an enhancement of identity, cancer was regarded with irrational revulsion, as a diminution of the self. There were also similar fictions of responsibility and of a characterological predisposition to the illness: cancer is regarded as a disease to which the psychically defeated, the inexpressive, the repressed—especially those who have repressed anger or sexual feelings— are particularly prone, as tuberculosis was regarded throughout the nineteenth and early twentieth centuries (indeed, until it was discovered how to cure it) as a disease apt to strike the hypersensitive, the talented, the passionate.

These parallels—between myths about tuberculosis to which we can all feel superior now, and superstitions about cancer still given credence by many cancer patients and their families—gave me the main strategy of a little book I decided to write about the mystifications surrounding cancer. I didn't think it would be useful—and I wanted to be useful—to tell yet one more story in the first person of how someone learned that she or he had cancer, wept, struggled, was comforted, suffered, took courage . . . though mine was also that story. A narrative, it seemed to me, would be less useful than an idea. For narrative pleasure I would appeal to other writers; and although more examples from literature immediately came to mind for the glamorous disease, tuberculosis, I found the diagnosis of cancer as a disease of those who have not really lived in such books as Tolstoy's "The Death of Ivan Ilyich," Arnold Bennett's *Riceyman Steps,* and Bernanos's *The Diary of a Country Priest.*

And so I wrote my book, wrote it very quickly, spurred by evangelical zeal as well as anxiety about how much time I had left to do any living or writing in. My aim was to alleviate unnecessary suffering—exactly as Nietzsche formulated it, in a passage in *Daybreak* that I came across recently:

> *Thinking about illness!*—To calm the imagination of the invalid, so that at least he should not, as hitherto, have to suffer more from thinking about his illness than from the illness itself—that, I

think, would be something! It would be a great deal!

The purpose of my book was to calm the imagination, not to incite it. Not to confer meaning, which is the traditional purpose of literary endeavor, but to deprive something of meaning: to apply that quixotic, highly polemical strategy, "against interpretation," to the real world this time. To the body. My purpose was, above all, practical. For it was my doleful observation, repeated again and again, that the metaphoric trappings that deform the experience of having cancer have very real consequences: they inhibit people from seeking treatment early enough, or from making a greater effort to get competent treatment. The metaphors and myths, I was convinced, kill. (For instance, they make people irrationally fearful of effective measures such as chemotherapy, and foster credence in thoroughly useless remedies such as diets and psychotherapy.) I wanted to offer other people who were ill and those who care for them an instrument to dissolve these metaphors, these inhibitions. I hoped to persuade terrified people who were ill to consult doctors, or to change their incompetent doctors for competent ones, who would give them proper care. To regard cancer as if it were just a disease—a very serious one, but just a disease. Not a curse, not a punishment, not an embarrassment. Without "meaning." And not necessarily a death sentence (one of the mystifications is that cancer = death). *Illness as Metaphor* is not just a polemic, it is an exhortation. I was saying: Get the doctors to tell you the truth; be an informed, active patient; find yourself good treatment, because good treatment does exist (amid the widespread ineptitude). Although *the* remedy does not exist, more than half of all cases can be cured by existing methods of treatment.

In the decade since I wrote *Illness as Metaphor*— and was cured of my own cancer, confounding my doctors' pessimism—attitudes about cancer have evolved. Getting cancer is not quite as much of a stigma, a creator of "spoiled identity" (to use Erving Goffman's expression). The word cancer is uttered more freely, and people are not often described anymore in obituaries as dying of a "very long illness." Although European and Japanese doctors still regularly impart a cancer diagnosis first to the family, and often counsel concealing it from the patient, American doctors have virtually abandoned this policy; indeed, a brutal announcement to the patient is now common. The new candor about cancer is part of the same obligatory candor (or lack of decorum) that brings us diagrams of the rectal-colon or genito-urinary tract ailments of our national leaders on television and on the front pages of newspapers—more and more it is precisely a virtue in our society to speak of what is supposed *not* to be named. The change can also be explained by the doctors' fear of lawsuits in a litigious society. And not least among the reasons that cancer is now treated less phobically, certainly with less secrecy, than a decade ago is that it is no longer the most feared disease. In recent years some of the onus of cancer has been lifted by the emergence of a disease whose charge of stigmatization, whose capacity to create spoiled identity, is far greater. It seems that societies need to have one illness which becomes identified with evil, and attaches blame to its "victims," but it is hard to be obsessed with more than one.

2

Just as one might predict for a disease that is not yet fully understood as well as extremely recalcitrant to treatment, the advent of this terrifying new disease, new at least in its epidemic form, has provided a large-scale occasion for the metaphorizing of illness.

Strictly speaking, AIDS—acquired immune deficiency syndrome—is not the name of an illness at all. It is the name of a medical condition, whose consequences are a spectrum of illnesses. In contrast to syphilis and cancer, which provide prototypes for most of the images and metaphors attached to AIDS, the very definition of AIDS requires the presence of other illnesses, so-called opportunistic infections and malignancies. But though not in *that* sense a single disease, AIDS lends itself to being regarded as one—in part because, unlike cancer and like syphilis, it is thought to have a single cause.

AIDS has a dual metaphoric genealogy. As a micro-process, it is described as cancer is: an invasion. When the focus is transmission of the disease, an older metaphor, reminiscent of syphilis, is invoked: pollution. (One gets it from the blood or sexual fluids of infected people or from contaminated blood products.) But the military metaphors used to describe AIDS have a somewhat different focus from those used in describing cancer. With cancer, the metaphor scants the issue of causality (still a murky topic in cancer research) and picks up at the point at which rogue cells inside the body mutate, eventually moving out from an original site or organ to overrun other organs or systems—a domestic subversion. In the description of AIDS the enemy is what causes the disease, an infectious agent that comes from the outside:

> The invader is tiny, about one sixteen-thousandth the size of the head of a pin. . . . Scouts of the body's immune system, large cells called macrophages, sense the presence of the diminutive foreigner and promptly alert the immune system. It begins to mobilize an array of cells that, among other things, produce antibodies to deal with the threat. Single-mindedly, the AIDS virus ignores many of the blood cells in its path, evades the rapidly advancing defenders and homes in on the master coordinator of the immune system, a helper T cell. . . .

This is the language of political paranoia, with its characteristic distrust of a pluralistic world. A defense system consisting of cells "that, among other things, produce antibodies to deal with the threat" is, predictably, no match for an invader who advances "single-mindedly." And the science-fiction flavor, already present in cancer talk, is even more pungent in accounts of AIDS—this one comes from *Time* magazine in late 1986—with infection described like the high-tech warfare for which we are being prepared (and inured) by the fantasies of our leaders and by video entertainments. In the era of Star Wars and Space Invaders, AIDS has proved an ideally comprehensible illness:

> On the surface of that cell, it finds a receptor into which one of its envelope proteins fits perfectly, like a key into a lock. Docking with the cell, the virus penetrates the cell membrane and is stripped of its protective shell in the process. . . .

Next the invader takes up permanent residence, by a form of alien takeover familiar in science-fiction narratives. The body's own cells *become* the invader. With the help of an enzyme the virus carries with it,

> the naked AIDS virus converts its RNA into . . . DNA, the master molecule of life. The molecule then penetrates the cell nucleus, inserts itself into a chromosome and takes over part of the cellular

machinery, directing it to produce more AIDS viruses. Eventually, overcome by its alien product, the cell swells and dies, releasing a flood of new viruses to attack other cells. . . .

As viruses attack other cells, runs the metaphor, so "a host of opportunistic diseases, normally warded off by a healthy immune system, attacks the body," whose integrity and vigor have been sapped by the sheer replication of "alien product" that follows the collapse of its immunological defenses. "Gradually weakened by the onslaught, the AIDS victim dies, sometimes in months, but almost always within a few years of the first symptoms." Those who have not already succumbed are described as "under assault, showing the telltale symptoms of the disease," while millions of others "harbor the virus, vulnerable at any time to a final, all-out attack."

Cancer makes cells proliferate; in AIDS, cells die. Even as this original model of AIDS (the mirror image of leukemia) has been altered, descriptions of how the virus does its work continue to echo the way the illness is perceived as infiltrating the society. "AIDS Virus Found to Hide in Cells, Eluding Detection by Normal Tests" was the headline of a recent front-page story in *The New York Times* announcing the discovery that the virus can "lurk" for years in the macrophages—disrupting their disease-fighting function without killing them, "even when the macrophages are filled almost to bursting with virus," and without producing antibodies, the chemicals the body makes in response to "invading agents" and whose presence has been regarded as an infallible marker of the syndrome.* That the virus isn't lethal for *all* the cells where it takes up residence, as is now thought, only increases the illness-foe's reputation for wiliness and invincibility.

What makes the viral assault so terrifying is that contamination, and therefore vulnerability, is understood as permanent. Even if someone infected were never to develop any symptoms—that is, the infection remained, or could by medical intervention be rendered, inactive—the viral enemy would be forever within. In fact, so it is believed, it is just a matter of time before something awakens ("triggers") it, before the appearance of "the telltale symptoms." Like syphilis, known to generations of doctors as "the great masquerader," AIDS is a clinical construction, an inference. It takes its identity from the presence of *some*

* The larger role assigned to the macrophages—"to serve as a reservoir for the AIDS virus because the virus multiplies in them but does not kill them, as it kills T-4 cells"—is said to explain the not uncommon difficulty of finding infected T-4 lymphocytes in patients who have antibodies to the virus and symptoms of AIDS. (It is still assumed that antibodies will develop once the virus spreads to these "key target" cells.) Evidence of presently infected populations of cells has been as puzzlingly limited or uneven as the evidence of infection in the populations of human societies—puzzling, because of the conviction that the disease is everywhere, and must spread. "Doctors have estimated that as few as one in a million T-4 cells are infected, which led some to ask where the virus hides. . . ." Another resonant speculation, reported in the same article (*The New York Times,* June 7, 1988): "Infected macrophages can transmit the virus to other cells, possibly by touching the cells."

among a long, and lengthening, roster of symptoms (no one has everything that AIDS could be), symptoms which "mean" that what the patient has is this illness. The construction of the illness rests on the invention not only of AIDS as a clinical entity but of a kind of junior AIDS, called AIDS-related complex (ARC), to which people are assigned if they show "early" and often intermittent symptoms of immunological deficit such as fevers, weight loss, fungal infections, and swollen lymph glands. AIDS is progressive, a disease of time. Once a certain density of symptoms is attained, the course of the illness can be swift, and brings atrocious suffering. Besides the commonest "presenting" illnesses (some hitherto unusual, at least in a fatal form, such as a rare skin cancer and a rare form of pneumonia), a plethora of disabling, disfiguring, and humiliating symptoms make the AIDS patient steadily more infirm, helpless, and unable to control or take care of basic functions and needs.

The sense in which AIDS is a slow disease makes it more like syphilis, which is characterized in terms of "stages," than like cancer. Thinking in terms of "stages" is essential to discourse about AIDS. Syphilis in its most dreaded form is "tertiary syphilis," syphilis in its third stage. What is called AIDS is generally understood as the last of three stages—the first of which is infection with a human immunodeficiency virus (HIV) and early evidence of inroads on the immune system—with a long latency period between infection and the onset of the "telltale" symptoms.

(Apparently not as long as syphilis, in which the latency period between secondary and tertiary illness might be decades. But it is worth noting that when syphilis first appeared in epidemic form in Europe at the end of the fifteenth century, it was a rapid disease, of an unexplained virulence that is unknown today, in which death often occurred in the second stage, sometimes within months or a few years.) Cancer *grows* slowly: it is not thought to be, for a long time, latent. (A convincing account of a process in terms of "stages" seems invariably to include the notion of a normative delay or halt in the process, such as is supplied by the notion of latency.) True, a cancer is "staged." This is a principal tool of diagnosis, which means classifying it according to its gravity, determining how "advanced" it is. But it is mostly a spatial notion: that the cancer advances through the body, traveling or migrating along predictable routes. Cancer is first of all a disease of the body's geography, in contrast to syphilis and AIDS, whose definition depends on constructing a temporal sequence of stages.

Syphilis is an affliction that didn't have to run its ghastly full course, to paresis (as it did for Baudelaire and Maupassant and Jules de Goncourt), and could and often did remain at the stage of nuisance, indignity (as it did for Flaubert). The scourge was also a cliché, as Flaubert himself observed. "SYPHILIS. Everybody has it, more or less" reads one entry in the *Dictionary of Accepted Opinions*, his treasury of mid-nineteenth-century platitudes. And syphilis did manage to acquire a darkly positive association in late-nineteenth- and early-twentieth-century Europe, when a link was made between syphilis and heightened ("feverish") mental activity that parallels the connection made since the era of the Romantic writers between pulmonary tuberculosis and heightened emotional activity. As if in honor of all the notable writers and artists who ended their lives in syphilitic witlessness, it came to be believed that the brain lesions of neurosyphilis might actually inspire original thought or art. Thomas Mann, whose fiction is a storehouse of early-twentieth-century disease myths, makes this notion of syphilis as muse central to his *Doctor Faustus*, with its protagonist a great composer whose voluntarily contracted syphilis—the Devil guarantees that the infection will be limited to the central nervous system—confers on him twenty-four years of incandescent creativity. E. M. Cioran recalls how, in Romania in the late 1920s, syphilis-envy figured in his adolescent expectations of literary glory: he would discover that he had contracted syphilis, be rewarded with several hyperproductive years of genius, then collapse into madness. This romanticizing of the dementia characteristic of neurosyphilis was the forerunner of the much more persistent fantasy in this century about mental illness as a source of artistic creativity or spiritual originality. But with AIDS—though dementia is also a common, late symptom—no compensatory mythology has arisen, or seems likely to arise. AIDS, like cancer, does not allow romanticizing or sentimentalizing, perhaps because its association with death is too powerful. In Krzysztof Zanussi's film *Spiral* (1978), the most truthful account I know of anger at dying, the protagonist's illness is never specified; therefore, it *has* to be cancer. For several generations now, the generic idea of death has been a death from cancer, and a cancer death is experienced as a generic defeat. Now the generic rebuke to life and to hope is AIDS.

3

Because of countless metaphoric flourishes that have made cancer synonymous with evil, having cancer has been experienced by many as shameful, therefore something to conceal, and also unjust, a betrayal by one's body. Why me? the cancer patient exclaims bitterly. With AIDS, the shame is linked to an imputation of guilt; and the scandal is not at all obscure. Few wonder, Why me? Most people outside of sub-Saharan Africa who have AIDS know (or think they know) how they got it. It is not a mysterious affliction that seems to strike at random. Indeed, to get AIDS is precisely to be revealed, in the majority of cases so far, as a member of a certain "risk group," a community of pariahs. The illness flushes out an identity that might have remained hidden from neighbors, job-mates, family, friends. It also confirms an identity and, among the risk group in the United States most severely affected in the beginning, homosexual men, has been a creator of community as well as an experience that isolates the ill and exposes them to harassment and persecution.

Getting cancer, too, is sometimes understood as the fault of someone who has indulged in "unsafe" behavior—the alcoholic with cancer of the esophagus, the smoker with lung cancer: punishment for living unhealthy lives. (In contrast to those obliged to perform unsafe occupations, like the worker in a petrochemical factory who gets bladder cancer.) More and more linkages are sought between primary organs or systems and specific practices that people are invited to repudiate, as in recent speculation associating colon cancer and breast cancer with diets rich in animal fats. But the unsafe habits associated with cancer, among other illnesses—even heart disease, hitherto little culpabilized, is now largely viewed as the price one pays for excesses of diet and "life-style"—are the result of a weakness of the will or a lack of prudence, or of addiction to legal (albeit very dangerous) chemicals. The unsafe behavior that produces AIDS is judged to be more than just weakness. It is indulgence, delinquency—addictions to chemicals that are illegal and to sex regarded as deviant.

The sexual transmission of this illness, considered by most people as a calamity one brings on oneself, is judged more harshly than other means—especially since AIDS is understood as a disease not only of sexual excess but of perversity. (I am thinking, of course, of the United States, where people are currently being told that heterosexual transmission is extremely rare, and unlikely—as if Africa did not exist.) An infectious disease whose principal means of transmission is sexual necessarily puts at greater risk those who are sexually more active—and is easy to view as a punishment for that activity. True of syphilis, this is even truer of AIDS, since not just promiscuity but a specific sexual "practice" regarded as unnatural is named as more endangering. Getting the disease through a sexual practice is thought to be more willful, therefore deserves more blame. Addicts who get the illness by sharing contaminated needles are seen as committing (or completing) a kind of inadvertent suicide. Promiscuous homosexual men practicing their vehement sexual customs under the illusory conviction, fostered by medical ideology with its cure-all antibiotics, of the relative innocuousness of all sexually transmitted diseases, could be viewed as dedicated hedonists—though it's now clear that their behavior was no less suicidal. Those like hemophiliacs and blood-transfusion recipients, who cannot by any stretch of the blaming faculty be considered responsible for their illness, may be as ruthlessly ostracized by frightened people, and potentially represent a greater threat because, unlike the already stigmatized, they are not as easy to identify.

Infectious diseases to which sexual fault is attached always inspire fears of easy contagion and bizarre fantasies of transmission by nonvenereal means in public places. The removal of doorknobs and the installation of swinging doors on U.S. Navy ships and the disappearance of the metal drinking cups affixed to public water fountains in the United States in the first decades of the century were early consequences of the "discovery" of syphilis's "innocently transmitted infection"; and the warning to generations of middle-class children always to interpose paper between bare bottom and the public toilet seat is another trace of the horror stories about the germs of syphilis being passed to the innocent by the dirty that were rife once and are still widely believed. Every feared epidemic disease, but especially those associated with sexual license, generates a preoccupying distinction between the disease's putative carriers (which usually means just the poor and, in this part of the world, people with darker skins) and those defined—health professionals and other bureaucrats do the defining—as "the general population." AIDS has revived similar phobias and fears of contamination among *this* disease's version of "the general population": white heterosexuals who do not inject themselves with drugs or have sexual relations with those who do. Like syphilis a disease of, or contracted from, dangerous others, AIDS is perceived as afflicting, in greater proportions than syphilis ever did, the already stigmatized. But syphilis was not identified with certain death, death that follows a protracted agony, as cancer was once imagined and AIDS is now held to be.

That AIDS is not a single illness but a syndrome, consisting of a seemingly open-ended list of contributing or "presenting" illnesses which constitute (that is, qualify the patient as having) the disease, makes it more a product of definition or construction than even a very complex, multiform illness like cancer. Indeed, the contention that AIDS is invariably fatal depends partly on what doctors decided to define as AIDS—and keep in reserve as distinct earlier stages of the disease. And this decision rests on a notion no less primitively metaphorical than that of a "full-blown" (or "full-fledged") disease.* "Full-blown" is the form in which

* The standard definition distinguishes between people with the disease or syndrome "fulfilling the criteria for the surveillance definition of AIDS" from a larger number infected with HIV and symptomatic "who do not fulfill the empiric criteria for the full-blown disease. This constellation of signs and symptoms in the context of HIV infection has been termed the AIDS-related complex (ARC)." Then follows the obligatory percentage. "It is estimated that approximately 25 percent of patients with ARC will develop full-blown disease within 3 years." Harrison's *Principles of Internal Medicine*, 11th edition (1987), p. 1394.

The first major illness known by an acronym, the condition called AIDS does not have, as it were, natural borders. It is an illness whose identity is designed for purposes of investigation and with tabulation and surveillance by medical and other bureaucracies in view. Hence, the unselfconscious equating in the medical textbook of what is empirical with what pertains to surveillance, two notions deriving from quite different models of understanding. (AIDS is what fulfills that which is referred to as either the "criteria for the surveillance definition" or the "empiric criteria": HIV infection plus the disease is inevitably fatal. As what is immature is destined to become mature, what buds to become full-blown (fledglings to become full-fledged)—the doctors' botanical or zoological metaphor makes development or evolution into AIDS the norm, the rule. I am not saying that the metaphor creates the clinical conception, but I am arguing that it does much more than just ratify it. It lends support to an interpretation of the clinical evidence which is far from proved or, yet, provable. It is simply too early to conclude, of a disease identified only seven years ago, that infection will always produce something to die from, or even that everybody who has what is defined as AIDS will die of it. (As some medical writers have speculated, the appalling mortality rates could be registering the early, mostly rapid deaths of those most vulnerable to the virus—because of diminished immune competence, because of genetic predisposition, among other possible co-factors—not the ravages of a uniformly fatal infection.) Construing the disease as divided into distinct stages was the necessary way of implementing the metaphor of "full-blown disease." But it also slightly weakened the notion of inevitability suggested by the metaphor. Those sensibly interested in hedging their bets about how uniformly

the presence of one or more diseases included on the roster drawn up by the disease's principal administrator of definition in the United States, the federal Centers for Disease Control in Atlanta.) This completely stipulative definition with its metaphor of maturing disease decisively influences how the illness is understood.

lethal infection would prove could use the standard three-tier classification—HIV infection, AIDS-related complex (ARC), and AIDS—to entertain either of two possibilities or both: the less catastrophic one, that *not* everybody infected would "advance" or "graduate" from HIV infection, and the more catastrophic one, that everybody would.

It is the more catastrophic reading of the evidence that for some time has dominated debate about the disease, which means that a change in nomenclature is under way. Influential administrators of the way the disease is understood have decided that there should be no more of the false reassurance that might be had from the use of different acronyms for different stages of the disease. (It could never have been more than minimally reassuring.) Recent proposals for re-doing terminology—for instance, to phase out the category of ARC—do not challenge the construction of the disease in stages, but do place additional stress on the *continuity* of the disease process. "Full-blown disease" is viewed as more inevitable now, and that strengthens the fatalism already in place.*

---

* The 1988 Presidential Commission on the epidemic recommended "de-emphasizing" the use of the term ARC because it "tends to obscure the life-threatening aspects of this stage of illness." There is some pressure to drop the term AIDS, too. The report by the Presidential Commission pointedly used the acronym HIV for the epidemic itself, as part of a recommended shift from "monitoring disease" to "monitoring infection." Again, one of the reasons given is that the present terminology masks the true gravity of the menace. ("This longstanding concentration on the clinical manifestations of AIDS rather than on all stages of HIV infection [i.e., from initial

From the beginning the construction of the illness had depended on notions that separated one group of people from another—the sick from the well, people with ARC from people with AIDS, them and us—while implying the imminent dissolution of these distinctions. However hedged, the predictions always sounded fatalistic. Thus, the frequent pronouncements by AIDS specialists and public health officials on the chances of those infected with the virus coming down with "full-blown" disease have seemed mostly an exercise in the management of public opinion, dosing out the harrowing news in several steps. Estimates of the percentage expected to show symptoms classifying them as having AIDS within five years, which may be too low—at the time of this writing, the figure is 30 to 35 percent—are invariably followed by the assertion that "most," after which comes "probably all," those infected will eventually become ill. The critical number, then, is not the percentage of people likely to develop AIDS within a relatively short time but the *maximum* interval that could elapse between infection with HIV (described as lifelong and irreversible) and appearance of the first symptoms. As the years add up in which the illness has been tracked, so does the possible num-

---

infection to seroconversion, to an antibody-positive asymptomatic stage, to full-blown AIDS] has had the unintended effect of misleading the public as to the extent of infection in the population. . . .") It does seem likely that the disease will, eventually, be renamed. *This* change in nomenclature would justify officially the policy of including the infected but asymptomatic among the ill.)

ber of years between infection and becoming ill, now estimated, seven years into the epidemic, at between ten and fifteen years. This figure, which will presumably continue to be revised upward, does much to maintain the definition of AIDS as an inexorable, invariably fatal disease.

The obvious consequence of believing that all those who "harbor" the virus will eventually come down with the illness is that those who test positive for it are regarded as people-with-AIDS, who just don't have it . . . yet. It is only a matter of time, like any death sentence. Less obviously, such people are often regarded as if they *do* have it. Testing positive for HIV (which usually means having been tested for the presence not of the virus but of antibodies to the virus) is increasingly equated with being ill. Infected *means* ill, from that point forward. "Infected but not ill," that invaluable notion of clinical medicine (the body "harbors" many infections), is being superseded by biomedical concepts which, whatever their scientific justification, amount to reviving the antiscientific logic of defilement, and make infected-but-healthy a contradiction in terms. Being ill in this new sense can have many practical consequences. People are losing their jobs when it is learned that they are HIV-positive (though it is not legal in the United States to fire someone for that reason) and the temptation to conceal a positive finding must be immense. The consequences of testing HIV-positive are even more punitive for those selected populations—there will be more

—upon which the government has already made testing mandatory. The U.S. Department of Defense has announced that military personnel discovered to be HIV-positive are being removed "from sensitive, stressful jobs," because of evidence indicating that mere infection with the virus, in the absence of any other symptoms, produces subtle changes in mental abilities in a significant minority of virus carriers. (The evidence cited: lower scores on certain neurological tests given to some who had tested positive, which could reflect mental impairment caused by exposure to the virus, though most doctors think this extremely improbable, or could be caused—as officially acknowledged under questioning—by "the anger, depression, fear, and panic" of people who have just learned that they are HIV-positive.) And, of course, testing positive now makes one ineligible to immigrate everywhere.

•

In every previous epidemic of an infectious nature, the epidemic is equivalent to the number of tabulated cases. This epidemic is regarded as consisting *now* of that figure plus a calculation about a much larger number of people apparently in good health (seemingly healthy, but doomed) who are infected. The calculations are being made and remade all the time, and pressure is building to identify these people, and to tag them. With the most up-to-date biomedical testing, it is possible to create a new class of lifetime pariahs, the future ill. But the result of this radical expansion of the notion of illness created by the triumph of modern medical scrutiny also seems a throwback to the past, before the era of medical triumphalism, when illnesses were innumerable, mysterious, and the progression from being seriously ill to dying was something normal (not, as now, medicine's lapse or failure, destined to be corrected). AIDS, in which people are understood as ill before they are ill; which produces a seemingly innumerable array of symptom-illnesses; for which there are only palliatives; and which brings to many a social death that precedes the physical one—AIDS reinstates something like a premodern experience of illness, as described in Donne's *Devotions*, in which "every thing that disorders a faculty and the function of that is a sicknesse," which starts when we

> are preafflicted, super-afflicted with these jelousies and suspitions, and apprehensions of Sicknes, before we can cal it a sicknes; we are not sure we are ill; one hand askes the other by the pulse, and our eye asks our own urine, how we do. . . . we are tormented with sicknes, and cannot stay till the torment come. . . .

whose agonizing outreach to every part of the body makes a real cure chimerical, since what "is but an accident, but a symptom of the main disease, is so violent, that the Phisician must attend the cure of that" rather than "the cure of the disease it self," and whose consequence is abandonment:

> As Sicknesse is the greatest misery, so the greatest misery of sicknes is solitude; when the infectious-nes of the disease deterrs them who should assist, from comming; even the Phisician dares scarse come. . . . it is an Outlawry, an Excommunication upon the patient. . . .

In premodern medicine, illness is described as it is experienced intuitively, as a relation of outside and inside: an interior sensation or something to be discerned on the body's surface, by sight (or just below, by listening, palpating), which is confirmed when the interior is opened to viewing (in surgery, in autopsy). Modern—that is, effective—medicine is characterized by far more complex notions of what is to be observed inside the body: not just the disease's results (damaged organs) but its cause (microorganisms), and by a far more intricate typology of illness.

In the older era of artisanal diagnoses, being examined produced an immediate verdict, immediate as the physician's willingness to speak. Now an examination means tests. And being tested introduces a time lapse that, given the unavoidably industrial character of competent medical testing, can stretch out for weeks: an agonizing delay for those who think they are awaiting a death sentence or an acquittal. Many are reluctant to be tested out of dread of the verdict, out of fear of being put on a list that could bring future discrimination or worse, and out of fatalism (what good would it do?). The usefulness of self-examination for the early detection of certain common cancers, much less likely to be fatal if treated before they are very advanced, is now widely understood. Early detection of an illness thought to be inexorable and incurable cannot seem to bring any advantage.

Like other diseases that arouse feelings of shame, AIDS is often a secret, but not from the patient. A cancer diagnosis was frequently concealed from patients by their families; an AIDS diagnosis is at least as often concealed from their families by patients. And as with other grave illnesses regarded as more than just illnesses, many people with AIDS are drawn to whole-body rather than illness-specific treatments, which are thought to be either ineffectual or too dangerous. (The disparagement of effective, scientific medicine for offering treatments that are *merely* illness-specific, and likely to be toxic, is a recurrent misconjecture of opinion that regards itself as enlightened.) This disastrous choice is still being made by some people with cancer, an illness that surgery and drugs can often cure. And a predictable mix of superstition and resignation is leading some people with AIDS to refuse antiviral chemotherapy, which, even in the absence of a cure, has proved of some effectiveness (in slowing down the syndrome's progress and in staving off some common presenting illnesses), and instead to seek to heal themselves, often under the auspices of some "alternative medicine" guru. But subjecting an emaciated body to the purification of a macrobiotic diet is about as helpful in treating AIDS as having oneself bled, the "holistic" medical treament of choice in the era of Donne.

4

Etymologically, patient means sufferer. It is not suffering as such that is most deeply feared but suffering that degrades.

That illness can be not only an epic of suffering but the occasion of some kind of self-transcendence is affirmed by sentimental literature and, more convincingly, by case histories offered by doctor-writers. Some illnesses seem more apt than others for this kind of meditation. Oliver Sacks uses catastrophic neurological illness as the material for his portraits of suffering and self-transcendence, diminishment and exaltation. His great forerunner, Sir Thomas Browne, used tuberculosis for a similar purpose, to ruminate about illness in general, in "A Letter to a Friend, Upon Occasion of the Death of his Intimate Friend" (1657), making pre-Romantic sense out of some of the familiar stereotypes about tuberculosis: that it is a distinctive manner of being ill ("this being a lingring Disease") and a distinctive manner of dying ("his soft Death"). A fiction about soft or easy deaths—in fact, dying of tuberculosis was often hard and extremely painful —is part of the mythology of most diseases that are not considered shameful or demeaning.

In contrast to the soft death imputed to tuberculosis, AIDS, like cancer, leads to a hard death. The metaphorized illnesses that haunt the collective imagination are all hard deaths, or envisaged as such. Being deadly is not in itself enough to produce terror. It is not even necessary, as in the puzzling case of leprosy, perhaps the most stigmatized of all diseases, although rarely fatal and extremely difficult to transmit. Cancer is more feared than heart disease, although someone who has had a coronary is more likely to die of heart disease in the next few years than someone who has cancer is likely to die of cancer. A heart attack is an event but it does not give someone a new identity, turning the patient into one of "them." It is not transforming, except in the sense of a transformation into something better: inspired by fear, the cardiac patient acquires good habits of exercise and diet, starts to lead a more prudent, healthier life. And it is often thought to produce, if only because it can be instantaneous, an easy death.

The most terrifying illnesses are those perceived not just as lethal but as dehumanizing, literally so. What was expressed in the rabies phobia of nineteenth-century France, with its countless pseudo-cases of contamination by animals newly turned "bestial" and even of "spontaneous" rabies (actual cases of rabies, *la rage*, were extremely rare), was the fantasy that infection transformed people into maddened animals—unleashing uncontrollable sexual, blasphemous impulses—not the fact that it was indeed, until Pasteur's discovery of a treatment in 1885, invariably fatal. And while cholera killed fewer people in Western Europe in the nineteenth century than smallpox did, it was more feared, because of the suddenness with which it struck and the indignity of the symptoms: fulminant diarrhea and vomiting, whose result anticipated the horror of post-mortem decomposition. Within several hours radical dehydration shrank the patient into a wizened caricature of his or her former self, the skin turned bluish-black (overwhelming, transfixing fear is still, in French, *une peur bleue*), the body became cold; death followed the same day or soon after.

Polio's effects could be horrifying—it withered the body—but it did not mark or rot the flesh: it was not repulsive. Further, polio affected the body only, though that may seem ruin enough, not the face. The relatively appropriate, unmetaphorical reaction to polio owes much to the privileged status of the face, so determining of our evaluation of physical beauty and of physical ruin. All the debunking of the Cartesian separation of *mind* and body by modern philosophy and modern science has not reduced by one iota this culture's conviction of the separation of *face* and body, which influences every aspect of manners, fashion, sexual appreciation, aesthetic sensibility—virtually all our notions of appropriateness. This separation is a main point of one of European culture's principal iconographical traditions, the depiction of Christian martyrdom, with its astounding schism between what is inscribed on the face and what is happening to the body. Those innumerable images of Saint Sebastian, Saint Agatha, Saint Lawrence (but not of Christ himself), with the face demonstrating its effortless superiority to the atrocious things that are being inflicted down there. Below, the ruin of the body. Above, a person, incarnated in the face, who looks away, usually up, not registering pain or fear; already elsewhere. (Only Christ, both Son of Man and Son of God, suffers in his face: has his Passion.) Our very notion of the person, of dignity, depends on the separation of face from body,* on the possibility that the face may be exempt, or exempt itself, from what is happening to the body. And however lethal, illnesses like heart attacks and influenza that do not damage or deform the face never arouse the deepest dread.

Not every kind of alteration to the face is perceived as repulsive or shaming. The most dreaded are those

---

* There can be no real argument against the aristocracy of the face, only some definitive raillery. An obsession with the pretentiousness of the division between face and body is central in Gombrowicz's *Ferdydurke*, which keeps reproposing that the body is parts, each with an independent life, and the face is just another body part. The point of view from which Gombrowicz launches his post-Rabelaisian satire on eros and on social class is that of an enforced, humiliating return to childhood—not of the enforced humiliations of illness. That is, Gombrowicz's novel is a comedy, not a tragedy.

that seem like mutations into animality (the leper's "lion face") or a kind of rot (as in syphilis). Underlying some of the moral judgments attached to disease are aesthetic judgments about the beautiful and the ugly, the clean and the unclean, the familiar and the alien or uncanny. (More accurately, these are judgments that originate before the stage at which aesthetic and moral categories split apart and, eventually, come to seem opposed.) What counts more than the amount of disfigurement is that it reflects underlying, ongoing changes, the dissolution of the person. Smallpox also disfigures, pitting the face; but the marks of smallpox don't get worse. Indeed, they are precisely the stigmata of a survivor. The marks on the face of a leper, a syphilitic, someone with AIDS are the signs of a progressive mutation, decomposition; something organic.

Sinister characterizations of the organic proliferated in the nineteenth century to describe both the disease and its cause. Specific diseases, such as cholera, as well as the state of being generally prone to illness, were thought to be caused by an "infected" (or "foul") atmosphere, effusions spontaneously generated from something unclean. Usually identified (first by its bad smell) as decaying organic matter, this disease-carrying atmosphere came to be identified with urban rather than rural squalor, and with garbage, rot, the proximity of cemeteries. These claims were eventually defeated by the discoveries by Pasteur and Koch of the role played by specific microorganisms. By 1880 the scientific community no longer believed in miasma, as these effusions were called, or in spontaneous generation. (In 1883, a year after Koch discovered the tubercle bacillus, he discovered the water-borne bacillus that causes cholera.) But even after the defeat of the miasmic theory by the germ theory of contagion, miasma lived on, shorn of its first-order causative status, as a kind of vague co-factor in the explanation of many illnesses. The conviction that living in dark, dirty cities causes (or at least produces a susceptibility to) tuberculosis is a version of the miasma theory, and continued to be given credence well into this century, long after the actual cause of tuberculosis had been discovered. It seems that something like what is supplied by miasma, the generalizing of infection into an atmosphere, is required to moralize a disease.

In the wake of its rejection by scientists, the theory inspired at least one great work of art: the opera Debussy made from Maeterlinck's play *Pelléas et Mélisande*, a sort of *Tristan und Isolde* relocated in the world of miasma. It is right that *Pelléas et Mélisande*, in which everyone avows feelings of weakness and being lost, and some are already ailing; with its old, decaying castle that lets in no light; where the ground is full of subterranean terrors and dank or watery depths into which one can fall—all the correlatives of miasma, minus the stench—seems, to us, supremely a portrait of *psychological* sickness, of neurosis. For precisely as the category of generic sickliness was phased out of nineteenth-century medical thinking by the new understanding of the extreme specificity of what causes illness, it migrated to the expanding domain of psychology. The physically sickly person became the neurasthenic or neurotic person. And the idea of an organically contaminated, objectively pathogenic environment reappeared in the notion of a psychologically contaminated ambiance that produced a disposition to mental illness.

The notion did not remain confined to the domain of psychology and, with psychology's new credibility as science, returned to reinfluence medicine. The widely held view that many or even most diseases are not "really" physical but mental (more conservatively, "psycho-somatic") perpetuates the form of the miasmic theory—with its surplus of causality, surplus of meaning—in a new version that has been extremely successful in the twentieth century. The theory that psychological miasma (depression, funk) can cause physical illness has been tried out with varying degrees of respectability on many diseases, including cancer. And one way in which AIDS, some of whose metaphors overlap those of cancer, seems very different from cancer, that illness saturated with distinctively modern evaluations of energy and of disaster, and is experienced as a throwback to premodern diseases like leprosy and syphilis, is that no one is tempted, not yet at least, to psychologize it.

5

"Plague" is the principal metaphor by which the AIDS epidemic is understood. And because of AIDS, the popular misidentification of cancer as an epidemic, even a plague, seems to be receding: AIDS has banalized cancer.

Plague, from the Latin *plaga* (stroke, wound), has long been used metaphorically as the highest standard of collective calamity, evil, scourge—Procopius, in his masterpiece of calumny, *The Secret History*, called the Emperor Justinian worse than the plague ("fewer escaped")—as well as being a general name for many frightening diseases. Although the disease to which the word is permanently affixed produced the most lethal of recorded epidemics, being experienced as a pitiless slayer is not necessary for a disease to be regarded as plague-like. Leprosy, very rarely fatal now, was not much more so when at its greatest epidemic strength, between about 1050 and 1350. And syphilis has been regarded as a plague—Blake speaks of "the youthful Harlot's curse" that "blights with plagues the Marriage hearse"—not because it killed often, but because it was disgracing, disempowering, disgusting.

It is usually epidemics that are thought of as plagues. And these mass incidences of illness are understood as inflicted, not just endured. Considering illness as a punishment is the oldest idea of what causes illness, and an idea opposed by all attention to the ill that deserves the noble name of medicine. Hippocrates, who wrote several treatises on epidemics, specifically ruled out "the wrath of God" as a cause of bubonic plague. But the illnesses interpreted in antiquity as punishments, like the plague in *Oedipus*, were not thought to be shameful, as leprosy and subsequently syphilis were to be. Diseases, insofar as they acquired meaning, were collective calamities, and judgments on a community. Only injuries and disabilities, not diseases, were thought of as individually merited. For an analogy in the literature of antiquity to the modern sense of a shaming, isolating disease, one would have to turn to Philoctetes and his stinking wound.

The most feared diseases, those that are not simply fatal but transform the body into something alienating, like leprosy and syphilis and cholera and (in the imagination of many) cancer, are the ones that seem particularly susceptible to promotion to "plague." Leprosy and syphilis were the first illnesses to be consistently described as repulsive. It was syphilis that, in the earliest descriptions by doctors at the end of the fifteenth century, generated a version of the metaphors that flourish around AIDS: of a disease that was not only repulsive and retributive but collectively invasive. Although Erasmus, the most influential European pedagogue of the early sixteenth century, described syphilis as "nothing but a kind of leprosy" (by 1529 he called it "something worse than leprosy"), it had already been understood as something different, because sexually transmitted. Paracelsus speaks (in Donne's paraphrase) of "that foule contagious disease which then had invaded mankind in a few places, and since overflowes in all, that for punishment of generall licentiousnes God first inflicted that disease." Thinking of syphilis as a punishment for an individual's transgression was for a long time, virtually until the disease became easily curable, not really distinct from regarding it as retribution for the licentiousness of a community—as with AIDS now, in the rich industrial countries. In contrast to cancer, understood in a modern way as a disease incurred by (and revealing of) individuals, AIDS is understood in a premodern way, as a disease incurred by people both as individuals and as members of a "risk group"—that neutral-sounding, bureaucratic category which also revives the archaic idea of a tainted community that illness has judged.

•

Not every account of plague or plague-like diseases, of course, is a vehicle for lurid stereotypes about illness and the ill. The effort to think critically, historically, about illness (about disaster generally) was attempted throughout the eighteenth century: say, from Defoe's *A Journal of the Plague Year* (1722) to Alessandro Manzoni's *The Betrothed* (1827). Defoe's historical fiction, purporting to be an eyewitness account of bubonic plague in London in 1665, does not further any understanding of the plague as punishment or, a later part of the script, as a transforming experience. And Manzoni, in his lengthy account of the passage of plague through the duchy of Milan in 1630, is avowedly committed to presenting a more accurate, less reductive view than his historical sources. But even these two complex narratives reinforce some of the perennial, simplifying ideas about plague.

One feature of the usual script for plague: the disease invariably comes from somewhere else. The names for syphilis, when it began its epidemic sweep through Europe in the last decade of the fifteenth century, are an exemplary illustration of the need to make a dreaded disease foreign.* It was the "French pox" to

* As noted in the first accounts of the disease: "This malady received from different peoples whom it affected different names," writes Giovanni di Vigo in 1514. Like earlier treatises on syphilis, written in Latin—by Nicolo Leoniceno (1497) and by Juan Almenar (1502)—the one by di Vigo calls it *morbus Gallicus*, the French disease. (Excerpts from this and other accounts of the period, including *Syphilis; Or a Poetical History of the French Disease* [1530] by Girolamo Fracastoro, who coined the name that prevailed, are in *Classic Descriptions of Disease*, edited by Ralph H. Major [1932].) Moralistic explanations abounded from the beginning. In 1495, a year after the epidemic started, the Emperor Maximilian issued an edict declaring syphilis to be an affliction from God for the sins of men.

The theory that syphilis came from even farther than a neighbor-the English, *morbus Germanicus* to the Parisians, the Naples sickness to the Florentines, the Chinese disease to the Japanese. But what may seem like a joke about the inevitability of chauvinism reveals a more important truth: that there is a link between imagining disease and imagining foreignness. It lies perhaps in the very concept of wrong, which is archaically identical with the non-us, the alien. A polluting person is always wrong, as Mary Douglas has observed. The inverse is also true: a person judged to be wrong is regarded as, at least potentially, a source of pollution.

The foreign place of origin of important illnesses, as of drastic changes in the weather, may be no more remote than a neighboring country. Illness is a species of invasion, and indeed is often carried by soldiers. Manzoni's account of the plague of 1630 (chapters 31 to 37) begins:

> The plague which the Tribunal of Health had feared might enter the Milanese provinces with the German troops had in fact entered, as is well known; and it is also well known that it did not stop there, but went on to invade and depopulate a large part of Italy.

---

ing country, that it was an entirely new disease in Europe, a disease of the New World brought back to the Old by sailors of Columbus who had contracted it in America, became the accepted explanation of the origin of syphilis in the sixteenth century and is still widely credited. It is worth noting that the earliest medical writers on syphilis did not accept the dubious theory. Leoniceno's *Libellus de Epidemia, quam vulgo morbum Gallicum vocant* starts by taking up the question of whether "the French disease under another name was common to the ancients," and says he believes firmly that it was.

Defoe's chronicle of the plague of 1665 begins similarly, with a flurry of ostentatiously scrupulous speculation about its foreign origin:

> It was about the beginning of September, 1664, that I, among the rest of my neighbours, heard in ordinary discourse that the plague was returned again in Holland; for it had been very violent there, and particularly at Amsterdam and Rotterdam, in the year 1663, whither, they say, it was brought, some said from Italy, others from the Levant, among some goods which were brought home by their Turkey fleet; others said it was brought from Candia; others from Cyprus. It mattered not from whence it came; but all agreed it was come into Holland again.

The bubonic plague that reappeared in London in the 1720s had arrived from Marseilles, which was where plague in the eighteenth century was usually thought to enter Western Europe: brought by seamen, then transported by soldiers and merchants. By the nineteenth century the foreign origin was usually more exotic, the means of transport less specifically imagined, and the illness itself had become phantasmagorical, symbolic.

At the end of *Crime and Punishment* Raskolnikov dreams of plague: "He dreamt that the whole world was condemned to a terrible new strange plague that had come to Europe from the depths of Asia." At the beginning of the sentence it is "the whole world," which turns out by the end of the sentence to be "Europe," afflicted by a lethal visitation from Asia. Dostoevsky's model is undoubtedly cholera, called Asiatic cholera, long endemic in Bengal, which had rapidly become and remained through most of the nineteenth century a worldwide epidemic disease. Part of the centuries-old conception of Europe as a privileged cultural entity is that it is a place which is colonized by lethal diseases coming from elsewhere. Europe is assumed to be by rights free of disease. (And Europeans have been astoundingly callous about the far more devastating extent to which they—as invaders, as colonists—have introduced *their* lethal diseases to the exotic, "primitive" world: think of the ravages of smallpox, influenza, and cholera on the aboriginal populations of the Americas and Australia.) The tenacity of the connection of exotic origin with dreaded disease is one reason why cholera, of which there were four great outbreaks in Europe in the nineteenth century, each with a lower death toll than the preceding one, has continued to be more memorable than smallpox, whose ravages increased as the century went on (half a million died in the European smallpox pandemic of the early 1870s) but which could not be construed as, plague-like, a disease with a non-European origin.

Plagues are no longer "sent," as in Biblical and Greek antiquity, for the question of agency has blurred. Instead, peoples are "visited" by plagues. And the visitations recur, as is taken for granted in the subtitle of Defoe's narrative, which explains that it is about that "which happened in London during the Last Great Visitation in 1665." Even for non-Europeans, lethal disease may be called a visitation. But a visitation on "them" is invariably described as different from one on "us." "I believe that about one half of the whole people was carried off by this visitation," wrote the English traveler Alexander Kinglake, reaching Cairo at a time of the bubonic plague (sometimes called "oriental plague"). "The Orientals, however, have more quiet fortitude than Europeans under afflictions of this sort." Kinglake's influential book *Eothen* (1844)—suggestively subtitled "Traces of Travel Brought Home from the East"—illustrates many of the enduring Eurocentric presumptions about others, starting from the fantasy that peoples with little reason to expect exemption from misfortune have a lessened capacity to *feel* misfortune. Thus it is believed that Asians (or the poor, or blacks, or Africans, or Muslims) don't suffer or don't grieve as Europeans (or whites) do. The fact that illness is associated with the poor—who are, from the perspective of the privileged, aliens in one's midst—reinforces the association of illness with the foreign: with an exotic, often primitive place.

Thus, illustrating the classic script for plague, AIDS is thought to have started in the "dark continent," then spread to Haiti, then to the United States and to Europe, then . . . It is understood as a tropical disease: another infestation from the so-called Third

World, which is after all where most people in the world live, as well as a scourge of the *tristes tropiques*. Africans who detect racist stereotypes in much of the speculation about the geographical origin of AIDS are not wrong. (Nor are they wrong in thinking that depictions of Africa as the cradle of AIDS must feed anti-African prejudices in Europe and Asia.) The subliminal connection made to notions about a primitive past and the many hypotheses that have been fielded about possible transmission from animals (a disease of green monkeys? African swine fever?) cannot help but activate a familiar set of stereotypes about animality, sexual license, and blacks. In Zaire and other countries in Central Africa where AIDS is killing tens of thousands, the counterreaction has begun. Many doctors, academics, journalists, government officials, and other educated people believe that the virus was sent to Africa from the United States, an act of bacteriological warfare (whose aim was to decrease the African birth rate) which got out of hand and has returned to afflict its perpetrators. A common African version of this belief about the disease's provenance has the virus fabricated in a CIA–Army laboratory in Maryland, sent from there to Africa, and brought back to its country of origin by American homosexual missionaries returning from Africa to Maryland.*

* The rumor may not have originated as a KGB-sponsored "disinformation" campaign, but it received a crucial push from Soviet propaganda specialists. In October 1985 the Soviet weekly *Litera-*

At first it was assumed that AIDS must become widespread elsewhere in the same catastrophic form in which it has emerged in Africa, and those who still think this will eventually happen invariably invoke the Black Death. The plague metaphor is an essential vehicle of the most pessimistic reading of the epidemiological prospects. From classic fiction to the latest journalism, the standard plague story is of inexorability, inescapability. The unprepared are taken by surprise; those observing the recommended precautions are struck down as well. *All* succumb when the story is told by an omniscient narrator, as in Poe's parable "The Masque of the Red Death" (1842), inspired by an account of a ball held in Paris during the cholera epidemic of 1832. Almost all—if the story

---

turnaya Gazeta published an article alleging that the AIDS virus had been engineered by the U.S. government during biological-warfare research at Fort Detrick, Maryland, and was being spread abroad by U.S. servicemen who had been used as guinea pigs. The source cited was an article in the Indian newspaper *Patriot*. Repeated on Moscow's "Radio Peace and Progress" in English, the story was taken up by newspapers and magazines throughout the world. A year later it was featured on the front page of London's conservative, mass-circulation *Sunday Express*. ("The killer AIDS virus was artificially created by American scientists during laboratory experiments which went disastrously wrong—and a massive cover-up has kept the secret from the world until today.") Though ignored by most American newspapers, the *Sunday Express* story was recycled in virtually every other country. As recently as the summer of 1987, it appeared in newspapers in Kenya, Peru, Sudan, Nigeria, Senegal, and Mexico. Gorbachev-era policies have since produced an official denial of the allegations by two eminent members of the Soviet Academy of Sciences, which was published in *Izvestia* in late October 1987. But the story is still being repeated—from Mexico to Zaire, from Australia to Greece.

is told from the point of view of a traumatized witness, who will be a benumbed survivor, as in Jean Giono's Stendhalian novel *Horseman on the Roof* (1951), in which a young Italian nobleman in exile wanders through cholera-stricken southern France in the 1830s.

•

Plagues are invariably regarded as judgments on society, and the metaphoric inflation of AIDS into such a judgment also accustoms people to the inevitability of global spread. This is a traditional use of sexually transmitted diseases: to be described as punishments not just of individuals but of a group ("generall licentiousnes"). Not only venereal diseases have been used in this way, to identify transgressing or vicious populations. Interpreting any catastrophic epidemic as a sign of moral laxity or political decline was as common until the later part of the last century as associating dreaded diseases with foreignness. (Or with despised and feared minorities.) And the assignment of fault is not contradicted by cases that do not fit. The Methodist preachers in England who connected the cholera epidemic of 1832 with drunkenness (the temperance movement was just starting) were not understood to be claiming that *everybody* who got cholera was a drunkard: there is always room for "innocent victims" (children, young women). Tuberculosis, in its identity as a disease of the poor (rather than of the "sensitive"), was also linked by late-nineteenth-century reformers to alcoholism. Responses to illnesses associated with sinners and the poor invariably recommended the adoption of middle-class values: the regular habits, productivity, and emotional self-control to which drunkenness was thought the chief impediment.* Health itself was eventually identified with these values, which were religious as well as mercantile, health being evidence of virtue as disease was of depravity. The dictum that cleanliness is next to godliness is to be taken quite literally. The succession of cholera epidemics in the nineteenth century shows a steady waning of religious interpretations of the disease; more precisely, these increasingly coexisted with other explanations. Although, by the time of the epidemic of 1866, cholera was commonly understood not simply as a divine punishment but as the consequence of remediable defects of sanitation, it was still regarded as the scourge of the sinful. A writer in *The New York Times* declared (April 22, 1866): "Cholera is especially the punishment of neglect of sanitary laws; it is the curse of the dirty, the intemperate, and the degraded." †

That it now seems unimaginable for cholera or a similar disease to be regarded in this way signifies not a

---

* According to the more comprehensive diagnosis favored by secular reformers, cholera was the result of poor diet and "indulgence in irregular habits." Officials of the Central Board of Health in London warned that there were no specific treatments for the disease, and advised paying attention to fresh air and cleanliness, though "the true preventatives are a healthy body and a cheerful, unruffled mind." Quoted in R. J. Morris, *Cholera 1832* (1976).

† Quoted in Charles E. Rosenberg, *The Cholera Years: The United States in 1832, 1849, and 1866* (1962).

lessened capacity to moralize about diseases but only a change in the kind of illnesses that are used didactically. Cholera was perhaps the last major epidemic disease fully qualifying for plague status for almost a century. (I mean cholera as a European and American, therefore a nineteenth-century, disease; until 1817 there had never been a cholera epidemic outside the Far East.) Influenza, which would seem more plague-like than any other epidemic in this century if loss of life were the main criterion, and which struck as suddenly as cholera and killed as quickly, usually in a few days, was never viewed metaphorically as a plague. Nor was a more recent epidemic, polio. One reason why plague notions were not invoked is that these epidemics did not have enough of the attributes perennially ascribed to plagues. (For instance, polio was construed as typically a disease of children—of the innocent.) The more important reason is that there has been a shift in the focus of the moralistic exploitation of illness. This shift, to diseases that can be interpreted as judgments on the individual, makes it harder to use epidemic disease as such. For a long time cancer was the illness that best fitted this secular culture's need to blame and punish and censor through the imagery of disease. Cancer was a disease of an individual, and understood as the result not of an action but rather of a failure to act (to be prudent, to exert proper self-control, or to be properly expressive). In the twentieth century it has become almost impossible to moralize about epidemics—except those which are transmitted sexually.

The persistence of the belief that illness reveals, and is a punishment for, moral laxity or turpitude can be seen in another way, by noting the persistence of descriptions of disorder or corruption as a disease. So indispensable has been the plague metaphor in bringing summary judgments about social crisis that its use hardly abated during the era when collective diseases were no longer treated so moralistically—the time between the influenza and encephalitis pandemics of the early and mid-1920s and the acknowledgment of a new, mysterious epidemic illness in the early 1980s—and when great infectious epidemics were so often and confidently proclaimed a thing of the past.* The plague metaphor was common in the 1930s as a synonym for social and psychic catastrophe. Evocations of plague of this type usually go with rant, with antiliberal attitudes: think of Artaud on theatre and plague, of Wilhelm Reich on "emotional plague." And such a generic "diagnosis" necessarily promotes antihistorical thinking. A theodicy as well as a demonology, it not only stipulates something emblematic of evil but makes this the bearer of a rough, terrible justice. In Karel Čapek's *The White Plague* (1937), the loathsome pestilence that has appeared in a state where fascism has come to power afflicts only those over the age of

* As recently as 1983, the historian William H. McNeill, author of *Plagues and Peoples*, started his review of a new history of the Black Death by asserting: "One of the things that separate us from our ancestors and make contemporary experience profoundly different from that of other ages is the disappearance of epidemic disease as a serious factor in human life" (*The New York Review of Books*, July 21, 1983). The Eurocentric presumption of this and many similar statements hardly needs pointing out.

forty, those who could be held morally responsible.

Written on the eve of the Nazi takeover of Czechoslovakia, Čapek's allegorical play is something of an anomaly—the use of the plague metaphor to convey the menace of what is defined as barbaric by a mainstream European liberal. The play's mysterious, grisly malady is something like leprosy, a rapid, invariably fatal leprosy that is supposed to have come, of course, from Asia. But Čapek is not interested in identifying political evil with the incursion of the foreign. He scores his didactic points by focusing not on the disease itself but on the management of information about it by scientists, journalists, and politicians. The most famous specialist in the disease harangues a reporter ("The disease of the hour, you might say. A good five million have died of it to date, twenty million have it and at least three times as many are going about their business, blithely unaware of the marble-like, marble-sized spots on their bodies"); chides a fellow doctor for using the popular terms, "the white plague" and "Peking leprosy," instead of the scientific name, "the Cheng Syndrome"; fantasizes about how his clinic's work on identifying the new virus and finding a cure ("every clinic in the world has an intensive research program") will add to the prestige of science and win a Nobel Prize for its discoverer; revels in hyperbole when it is thought a cure has been found ("it was the most dangerous disease in all history, worse than the bubonic plague"); and outlines plans for sending those with symptoms to well-guarded detention camps ("Given that every carrier of the disease is a potential spreader of the disease, we *must* protect the uncontaminated from the contaminated. All sentimentality in this regard is fatal and therefore criminal"). However cartoonish Čapek's ironies may seem, they are a not improbable sketch of catastrophe (medical, ecological) as a managed public event in modern mass society. And however conventionally he deploys the plague metaphor, as an agency of retribution (in the end the plague strikes down the dictator himself), Čapek's feel for public relations leads him to make explicit in the play the understanding of disease *as* a metaphor. The eminent doctor declares the accomplishments of science to be as nothing compared with the merits of the dictator, about to launch a war, "who has averted a far worse scourge: the scourge of anarchy, the leprosy of corruption, the epidemic of barbaric liberty, the plague of social disintegration fatally sapping the organism of our nation."

Camus's *The Plague*, which appeared a decade later, is a far less literal use of plague by another great European liberal, as subtle as Čapek's *The White Plague* is schematic. Camus's novel is not, as is sometimes said, a political allegory in which the outbreak of bubonic plague in a Mediterranean port city represents the Nazi occupation. This plague is not retributive. Camus is not protesting anything, not corruption or tyranny, not even mortality. The plague is no more or less than an exemplary event, the irruption of death that gives life its seriousness. His use of plague, more epitome than metaphor, is detached, stoic, aware—it is not about bringing judgment. But, as in Čapek's play, characters in Camus's novel declare how unthinkable it is to have a plague in the twentieth century . . . as if the belief that such a calamity could not happen, could not happen *anymore*, means that it must.

6

The emergence of a new catastrophic epidemic, when for several decades it had been confidently assumed that such calamities belonged to the past, would not be enough to revive the moralistic inflation of an epidemic into a "plague." It was necessary that the epidemic be one whose most common means of transmission is sexual.

Cotton Mather called syphilis a punishment "which the Just Judgment of God has reserved for our Late Ages." Recalling this and other nonsense uttered about syphilis from the end of the fifteenth to the early twentieth centuries, one should hardly be surprised that many want to view AIDS metaphorically—as, plaguelike, a moral judgment on society. Professional fulminators can't resist the rhetorical opportunity offered by a sexually transmitted disease that is lethal. Thus, the fact that AIDS is predominantly a heterosexually transmitted illness in the countries where it first emerged in epidemic form has not prevented such guardians of public morals as Jesse Helms and Norman Podhoretz from depicting it as a visitation specially aimed at (and deservedly incurred by) Western homosexuals, while another Reagan-era celebrity, Pat Buchanan, orates about "AIDS and Moral Bankruptcy," and Jerry Falwell offers the generic diagnosis that "AIDS is God's judgment on a society that does not live by His rules." What is surprising is not that the AIDS epidemic has been exploited in this way but that such cant has been confined to so predictable a sector of bigots; the official discourse about AIDS invariably includes admonitions against bigotry.

The pronouncements of those who claim to speak for God can mostly be discounted as the rhetoric regularly prompted by sexually transmitted illness—from Cotton Mather's judgment to recent statements by two leading Brazilian clerics, Bishop Falcão of Brasilia, who declares AIDS to be "the consequence of moral decadence," and the Cardinal of Rio de Janeiro, Eugenio Sales, who wants it both ways, describing AIDS as "God's punishment" and as "the revenge of nature." More interesting, because their purposes are more complex, are the secular sponsors of this sort of invective. Authoritarian political ideologies have a vested interest in promoting fear, a sense of the imminence of takeover by aliens—and real diseases are useful material. Epidemic diseases usually elicit a call to ban the entry of foreigners, immigrants. And xenophobic propaganda has always depicted immigrants as bearers of disease (in the late nineteenth century: cholera, yellow fever, typhoid fever, tuberculosis). It seems logical that the political figure in France who represents the most extreme nativist, racist views, Jean-Marie Le Pen, has attempted a strategy of fomenting fear of this new alien peril, insisting that AIDS is not just infectious but contagious, and calling for mandatory nationwide testing and the quarantine of everyone carrying the virus. And AIDS is a gift to the present regime in South Africa, whose Foreign Minister declared recently, evoking the incidence of the illness among the mine workers imported from neighboring all-black countries: "The terrorists are now coming to us with a weapon more terrible than Marxism: AIDS."

The AIDS epidemic serves as an ideal projection for First World political paranoia. Not only is the so-called AIDS virus the quintessential invader from the Third World. It can stand for any mythological menace. In this country, AIDS has so far evoked less pointedly racist reactions than in Europe, including the Soviet Union, where the African origin of the disease is stressed. Here it is as much a reminder of feelings associated with the menace of the Second World as it is an image of being overrun by the Third. Predictably, the public voices in this country most committed to drawing moral lessons from the

AIDS epidemic, such as Norman Podhoretz, are those whose main theme is worry about America's will to maintain its bellicosity, its expenditures on armaments, its firm anti-communist stance, and who find everywhere evidence of the decline of American political and imperial authority. Denunciations of "the gay plague" are part of a much larger complaint, common among antiliberals in the West and many exiles from the Russian bloc, about contemporary permissiveness of all kinds: a now-familiar diatribe against the "soft" West, with its hedonism, its vulgar sexy music, its indulgence in drugs, its disabled family life, which have sapped the will to stand up to communism. AIDS is a favorite concern of those who translate their political agenda into questions of group psychology: of national self-esteem and self-confidence. Although these specialists in ugly feelings insist that AIDS is a punishment for deviant sex, what moves them is not just, or even principally, homophobia. Even more important is the utility of AIDS in pursuing one of the main activities of the so-called neoconservatives, the Kulturkampf against all that is called, for short (and inaccurately), the 1960s. A whole politics of "the will"—of intolerance, of paranoia, of fear of political weakness—has fastened on this disease.

AIDS is such an apt goad to familiar, consensus-building fears that have been cultivated for several generations, like fear of "subversion"—and to fears that have surfaced more recently, of uncontrollable pollution and of unstoppable migration from the Third World—that it would seem inevitable that AIDS be envisaged in this society as something total, civilization-threatening. And raising the disease's metaphorical stature by keeping alive fears of its easy transmissibility, its imminent spread, does not diminish its status as, mainly, a consequence of illicit acts (or of economic and cultural backwardness). That it is a punishment for deviant behavior and that it threatens the innocent—these two notions about AIDS are hardly in contradiction. Such is the extraordinary potency and efficacy of the plague metaphor: it allows a disease to be regarded both as something incurred by vulnerable "others" and as (potentially) everyone's disease.

Still, it is one thing to emphasize how the disease menaces everybody (in order to incite fear and confirm prejudice), quite another to argue (in order to defuse prejudice and reduce stigma) that eventually AIDS will, directly or indirectly, affect everybody. Recently these same mythologists who have been eager to use AIDS for ideological mobilization against deviance have backed away from the most panic-inspiring estimates of the illness. They are among the most vocal of those who insist that infection will *not* spread to "the general population" and have turned their attention to denouncing "hysteria" or "frenzy" about AIDS. Behind what they now consider the excessive publicity given the disease, they discern the desire to placate an all-powerful minority by agreeing to regard "their" disease as "ours"—further evidence of ecause AIDS is not only invasive (a trait it shares with cancer) or even because it is infectious, but because of the specific imagery that surrounds viruses.

Virology supplies a new set of medical metaphors independent of AIDS which nevertheless reinforce the AIDS mythology. It was years before AIDS that William Burroughs oracularly declared, and Laurie Anderson echoed, "Language is a virus." And the viral explanation is invoked more and more often. Until recently, most of the infections recognized as viral were ones, like rabies and influenza, that have very rapid effects. But the category of slow-acting viral infections is growing. Many progressive and invariably fatal disorders of the central nervous system and some degenerative diseases of the brain that can appear in old age, as well as the so-called auto-immune diseases, are now suspected of being, in fact, slow virus diseases. (And evidence continues to accumulate for a viral cause of at least some human cancers.) Notions of conspiracy translate well into metaphors of implacable, insidious, infinitely patient viruses. In contrast to bacteria, which are relatively complex organisms, viruses are described as an extremely primitive form of life. At the same time, their activities are far more complex than those envisaged in the earlier germ models of infection. Viruses are not simply agents of infection, contamination. They transport genetic "information," they transform cells. And they themselves, many of them, evolve. While the smallpox virus appears to stay constant for centuries, influenza viruses evolve so rapidly

the sway of nefarious "liberal" values and of America's spiritual decline. Making AIDS everyone's problem and therefore a subject on which everyone needs to be educated, charge the antiliberal AIDS mythologists, subverts our understanding of the difference between "us" and "them"; indeed, exculpates or at least makes irrelevant moral judgments about "them." (In such rhetoric the disease continues to be identified almost exclusively with homosexuality, and specifically the practice of sodomy.) "Has America become a country where classroom discussion of the Ten Commandments is impermissible but teacher instructions in safe sodomy are to be mandatory?" inquires Pat Buchanan, protesting the "foolish" proposal made in the report of the recent Presidential Commission on the epidemic, chaired by Admiral Watkins, to outlaw discrimination against people with AIDS. Not the disease but the appeals heard from the most official quarters "to set aside prejudice and fear in favor of compassion" (the words of the Watkins Report) have become a principal target, suggesting as they do a weakening of this society's power (or willingness) to punish and segregate through judgments about sexual behavior.

•

More than cancer, but rather like syphilis, AIDS seems to foster ominous fantasies about a disease that is a marker of both individual and social vulnerabilities. The virus invades the body; the disease (or, in the newer version, the fear of the disease) is described as invading the whole society. In late 1986 President Reagan pronounced AIDS to be spreading— "insidiously" of course—"through the length and breadth of our society."* But AIDS, while the pretext for expressing dark intimations about the body politic, has yet to seem credible as a political metaphor for internal enemies, even in France, where AIDS—in French *le sida*—was quickly added to the store of political invective. Le Pen has dismissed some of his opponents as "AIDS-ish" (*sidatique*), and the antiliberal polemicist Louis Pauwels said that lycée students on strike last year were suffering from "mental AIDS" (*sont atteint d'un sida mental*). Neither has AIDS proved of much use as a metaphor for international political evil. True, Jeane Kirkpatrick once couldn't resist comparing international terrorism to AIDS, but such sallies are rare—perhaps because for that purpose the cancer metaphor has proved so fecund.

This doesn't mean that AIDS is not used, preposterously, as a metaphor, but only that AIDS has a metaphoric potential different from that of cancer. When the movie director in Alain Tanner's film *La Vallée Fantôme* (1987) muses, "Cinema is like a cancer," and then corrects himself, "No, it's

* Reagan's affirmation through cliché of the frightening reality of a disease of other people contrasts with his more original denial of the reality of his own illness. When asked how he felt after his cancer operation, he declared: "I didn't have cancer. I had something inside of me that had cancer in it and it was removed."

· 66 ·

infectious, it's more like AIDS," the c[...] lumberingly self-conscious as well as a[...] use of AIDS. Not its infectiousness but i[...] latency offers a more distinctive use of A[...] phor. Thus, the Palestinian Israeli writer[...] mas in the Jerusalem weekly *Kol Ha'i[...] medical, sexual, and political fantasy,[...] scribed Israel's Declaration of Independen[...]

the AIDS of "the Jewish State in the[...] Israel," whose long incubation has p[...] Gush Emunim and . . . [Rabbi Meir] l[...] That is where it all began, and that is whe[...] will end. AIDS, I am sorry to say, despi[...] sympathy for homosexuals, affects mainly [...] erotics, and a mononational Jewish State co[...] by definition the seeds of its own destruction[...] collapse of the political immune system tha[...] call democracy. . . . Rock Hudson, who once[...] as beautiful as a Palmachnik, now lies dying l[...] after the dissolution of the Palmach. The St[...] of Israel (for Jews, of course) was indeed on[...] beautiful. . . .

And even more promising than its connection w[...] latency is the potential of AIDS as a metaphor f[...] contamination and mutation. Cancer is still commo[...] as a metaphor for what is feared or deplored, even i[...] the illness is less dreaded than before. If AIDS can[...] eventually be drafted for comparable use, it will be[...]

· 67 ·

that vaccines need to be modified every year to keep up with changes in the "surface coat" of the virus.* The virus or, more accurately, viruses thought to cause AIDS are at least as mutable as the influenza viruses. Indeed, "virus" is now a synonym for change. Linda Ronstadt, recently explaining why she prefers doing Mexican folk music to rock 'n' roll, observed: "We don't have any tradition in contemporary music except change. Mutate, like a virus."

So far as "plague" still has a future as a metaphor, it is through the ever more familiar notion of the virus. (Perhaps no disease in the future caused by a bacillus will be considered as plague-like.) Information itself, now inextricably linked to the powers of computers, is threatened by something compared to a virus. Rogue or pirate programs, known as software viruses, are described as paralleling the behavior of biological viruses (which can capture the genetic code of parts of an organism and effect transfers of alien genetic material). These programs, deliberately planted onto a floppy disk meant to be used with the computer or introduced when the computer is communicating over

* The reason that a vaccine is considered the optimal response to viruses has to do with what makes them "primitive." Bacteria have many metabolic differences from mammalian cells and can reproduce outside the cells of their host, which makes it possible to find substances that target them specifically. With viruses, which bond with their host cells, it is a much more difficult problem to distinguish viral functions from normal cellular ones. Hence, the main strategy for controlling viral infections has been the development of vaccines, which do not "attack" a virus directly (as penicillin attacks infectious bacteria) but "forestall" infection by stimulating the immune system in advance.

telephone lines or data networks with other computers, copy themselves onto the computer's operating system. Like their biological namesakes, they won't produce immediate signs of damage to the computer's memory, which gives the newly "infected" program time to spread to other computers. Such metaphors drawn from virology, partly stimulated by the omnipresence of talk of AIDS, are turning up everywhere. (The virus that destroyed a considerable amount of data at the student computer center at Lehigh University in Bethlehem, Pennsylvania, in 1987, was given the name PC AIDS. In France, computer specialists already speak of the problem of *le sida informatique*.) And they reinforce the sense of the omnipresence of AIDS.

It is perhaps not surprising that the newest transforming element in the modern world, computers, should be borrowing metaphors drawn from our newest transforming illness. Nor is it surprising that descriptions of the course of viral infection now often echo the language of the computer age, as when it is said that a virus will normally produce "new copies of itself." In addition to the mechanistic descriptions, the way viruses are animistically characterized—as a menace in waiting, as mutable, as furtive, as biologically innovative—reinforces the sense that a disease can be something ingenious, unpredictable, novel. These metaphors are central to ideas about AIDS that distinguish this illness from others that have been regarded as plague-like. For though the fears

AIDS represents are old, its status as that unexpected
event, an entirely new disease—a new judgment, as it
were—adds to the dread.

7

Some will allow no Diseases to be new, others
think that many old ones are ceased; and that
such which are esteemed new, will have but their
time: However, the Mercy of God hath scat-
tered the great heap of Diseases, and not loaded
any one Country with all: some may be new in
one Country which have been old in another.
New Discoveries of the Earth discover new Diseases . . . and if Asia, Africa, and America should
bring in their List, Pandoras Box would swell,
and there must be a strange Pathology.
> —Sir Thomas Browne, "A Letter
> to a Friend, Upon Occasion of
> the Death of his Intimate Friend"

It is, of course, unlikely that AIDS, first identified
in the early 1980s, is a new disease. Most probably
the virus has been around a long time, and not only
in Africa, though it is only recently (and in Africa)

that the disease has attained epidemic volume. But for general consciousness it *is* a new disease, and for medicine, too: AIDS marks a turning point in current attitudes toward illness and medicine, as well as toward sexuality and toward catastrophe. Medicine had been viewed as an age-old military campaign now nearing its final phase, leading to victory. The emergence of a new epidemic disease, when for several decades it had been confidently assumed that such calamities belonged to the past, has inevitably changed the status of medicine. The advent of AIDS has made it clear that the infectious diseases are far from conquered and their roster far from closed.

Medicine changed mores. Illness is changing them back. Contraception and the assurance by medicine of the easy curability of sexually transmitted diseases (as of almost all infectious diseases) made it possible to regard sex as an adventure without consequences. Now AIDS obliges people to think of sex as having, possibly, the direst consequences: suicide. Or murder. (There was a trial run for the conversion of sexuality to something dangerous in the widely diffused panic about herpes in the United States in the early 1980s— and herpes in most cases is merely awful, erotically disqualifying.) The fear of AIDS imposes on an act whose ideal is an experience of pure presentness (and a creation of the future) a relation to the past to be ignored at one's peril. Sex no longer withdraws its partners, if only for a moment, from the social. It cannot be considered just a coupling; it is a chain, a chain of transmission, from the past. "So remember when a person has sex, they're not just having it with that partner, they're having it with everybody that partner had it with for the past ten years," runs an endearingly gender-vague pronouncement made in 1987 by the Secretary of Health and Human Services, Dr. Otis R. Bowen. AIDS reveals all but long-term monogamous sex as promiscuous (therefore dangerous) and also as deviant, for all heterosexual relations are also homosexual ones, once removed.

Fear of sexuality is the new, disease-sponsored register of the universe of fear in which everyone now lives. Cancerphobia taught us the fear of a polluting environment; now we have the fear of polluting people that AIDS anxiety inevitably communicates. Fear of the Communion cup, fear of surgery: fear of contaminated blood, whether Christ's blood or your neighbor's. Life—blood, sexual fluids—is itself the bearer of contamination. These fluids are potentially lethal. Better to abstain. People are storing their own blood, for future use. The model of altruistic behavior in our society, giving blood anonymously, has been compromised, since no one can be sure about anonymous blood received. Not only does AIDS have the unhappy effect of reinforcing American moralism about sex; it further strengthens the culture of self-interest, which is much of what is usually praised as "individualism." Self-interest now receives an added boost as simple medical prudence.

All rapid epidemics, including those in which there

is no suspicion of sexual transmission or any culpabiliz-
ing of the ill, give rise to roughly similar practices of
avoidance and exclusion. In the influenza pandemic
of 1918–19—influenza is a highly communicable disease, caused by an airborne virus (transmitted via the
respiratory system)—people were advised against shak-
ing hands and urged to put handkerchiefs over their
mouths when kissing. Police officers were ordered to
don gauze masks before entering a house where people
had become ill, as many police officers do today when
making arrests in the lower depths, since AIDS in the
United States has become increasingly a disease of the
urban poor, particularly blacks and Hispanics. Many
barbers and dentists wore masks and gloves, as dentists
and dental hygienists do now. But the great influenza
epidemic, which killed twenty million people, was an
affair of fifteen months. With a slow-motion epidemic, these same precautions take on a life of their
own. They become part of social mores, not a practice
adopted for a brief period of emergency, then dis-
carded.

With an epidemic in which there is no immediate
prospect of a vaccine, much less of a cure, prevention
plays a larger part in consciousness. But campaigns to
keep people from getting ill run into many difficulties
with diseases that are venereally transmitted. There has
always been reluctance in American health campaigns
to communicate information about ways of having
safer sex. The *U.S. Guide for Schools* issued in late
1987 by the Department of Education virtually refuses

to discuss reducing risk and proposes abstinence as the best way of safeguarding against AIDS, recalling lectures given soldiers during World War I that chastity was the only safeguard against syphilis as well as part of their patriotic duty in fighting the Hun.* Talk of condoms and clean needles is felt to be tantamount to condoning and abetting illicit sex, illegal chemicals. (And to some extent is. Education about how to keep from getting AIDS does imply an acknowledgment of, therefore tolerance of, the ineradicable variousness of expression of sexual feeling.) European societies, less committed to sexual hypocrisy at the level of public edict, are unlikely to urge people to be chaste as a way of warning them to be prudent. "Be careful. AIDS." And "AIDS. Don't die of ignorance." The specific meaning of these generalities to be seen on billboards and television spots throughout Western Europe for several years is: Use condoms. But there is a larger meaning in all these messages about being careful, not being ignorant, that will facilitate the acceptance of this kind of public service ad

* The other side of this refusal to give instructions about practices that would be less risky was the feeling that it was less than manly to submit one's sexual life to the guidelines of safety and prudence. According to Hemingway's fantasy, in *Death in the Afternoon* (1932): "Syphilis was the disease of the crusaders in the middle ages. It was supposed to be brought to Europe by them, and it is a disease of all people who lead lives in which disregard of consequences dominates. It is an industrial accident, to be expected by all those who lead irregular sexual lives and from their habits of mind would rather take chances than use prophylactics, and it is a to-be-expected end, or rather phase, of the life of all fornicators who continue their careers far enough."

here as well. Part of making an event real is just *saying* it, over and over. In this case, to say it over and over is to instill the consciousness of risk, the necessity of prudence as such, prior to and superseding any specific recommendation.

•

Of course, between the perennial official hypocrisy and the fashionable libertinism of recent decades there is a vast gap. The view that sexually transmitted diseases are not serious reached its apogee in the 1970s, which was also when many male homosexuals reconstituted themselves as something like an ethnic group, one whose distinctive folkloric custom was sexual voracity, and the institutions of urban homosexual life became a sexual delivery system of unprecedented speed, efficiency, and volume. Fear of AIDS enforces a much more moderate exercise of appetite, and not just among homosexual men. In the United States sexual behavior pre-1981 now seems for the middle class part of a lost age of innocence—innocence in the guise of licentiousness, of course. After two decades of sexual spending, of sexual speculation, of sexual inflation, we are in the early stages of a sexual depression. Looking back on the sexual culture of the 1970s has been compared to looking back on the jazz age from the wrong side of the 1929 crash.

One set of messages of the society we live in is: Consume. Grow. Do what you want. Amuse yourselves. The very working of this economic system, which has bestowed these unprecedented liberties, most cherished in the form of physical mobility and material prosperity, depends on encouraging people to defy limits. Appetite is *supposed* to be immoderate. The ideology of capitalism makes us all into connoisseurs of liberty—of the indefinite expansion of possibility. Virtually every kind of advocacy claims to offer first of all or also some increment of freedom. Not every freedom, to be sure. In rich countries, freedom has come to be identified more and more with "personal fulfillment"—a freedom enjoyed or practiced alone (or *as* alone). Hence much of recent discourse about the body, reimagined as the instrument with which to enact, increasingly, various programs of self-improvement, of the heightening of powers. Given the imperatives about consumption and the virtually unquestioned value attached to the expression of self, how could sexuality *not* have come to be, for some, a consumer option: an exercise of liberty, of increased mobility, of the pushing back of limits. Hardly an invention of the male homosexual subculture, recreational, risk-free sexuality is an inevitable reinvention of the culture of capitalism, and was guaranteed by medicine as well. The advent of AIDS seems to have changed all that, irrevocably.

AIDS magnifies the force of the quite different yet complementary messages increasingly heard by people in this society accustomed to being able to provide pleasures for themselves, more and more of whom are drawn to programs of self-management and self-discipline (diet, exercise). Watch your appetites. Take care of yourself. Don't let yourself go. Limits have long been set on the indulgence of certain appetites in the name of health or of the creation of an ideal physical appearance—voluntary limits, an exercise of freedom. The catastrophe of AIDS suggests the immediate *necessity* of limitation, of constraint for the body and for consciousness. But the response to AIDS is more than reactive, more than a fearful and therefore appropriate response to a very real danger. It also expresses a positive desire, the desire for stricter limits in the conduct of personal life. There is a broad tendency in our culture, an end-of-an-era feeling, that AIDS is reinforcing; an exhaustion, for many, of purely secular ideals—ideals that seemed to encourage libertinism or at least not provide any coherent inhibition against it—in which the response to AIDS finds its place. The behavior AIDS is stimulating is part of a larger grateful return to what is perceived as "conventions," like the return to figure and landscape, tonality and melody, plot and character, and other much vaunted repudiations of difficult modernism in the arts. The reduction in the imperative of promiscuity in the middle class, a growth of the ideal of monogamy, of a prudent sexual life, is as marked in, say, Stockholm, with its tiny number of AIDS cases, as it is in New York, where the disease can accurately be called of epidemic proportions. The response to AIDS, while in part perfectly rational, amplifies a widespread questioning that had been rising in intensity throughout the 1970s of many of the ideals (and risks) of enlightened modernity; and the new sexual realism goes with the rediscovery of the joys of tonal music, Bouguereau, a career in investment banking, and church weddings.

The mounting panic about the risks of recreational and commercialized sexuality is unlikely to diminish the attractions of other kinds of appetites: boutiques are expected to fill the building in Hamburg until recently occupied by the Eros Center. Sexual exchanges are to be carried out only after forethought. Routine consumption of drugs that boosted energies for mental work and for palaver (what also rose throughout the 1970s was bourgeois cocaine use) has played its part in preparing for the neo-celibacy and waning of sexual spontaneity common among the educated in this decade. Machines supply new, popular ways of inspiring desire and keeping it safe, as mental as possible: the commercially organized lechery by telephone (and in France by "Minitel") that offers a version of anonymous promiscuous sex without the exchange of fluids. And strictures about contact now have their place in the computer world as well. Computer users are advised to regard each new piece of software as a "potential carrier" of a virus. "Never put a disk in your computer without verifying its source." The so-called vaccine programs being marketed are said to offer some protection; but the only sure way to curb the threat of computer viruses, experts agree, is not to share programs and data. The culture of consumption may actually be stimulated by the warnings to consumers of all kinds of goods and services to be more cautious, more selfish. For these anxieties will require the further replication of goods and services.

8

Epidemics of particularly dreaded illnesses always provoke an outcry against leniency or tolerance—now identified as laxity, weakness, disorder, corruption: unhealthiness. Demands are made to subject people to "tests," to isolate the ill and those suspected of being ill or of transmitting illness, and to erect barriers against the real or imaginary contamination of foreigners. Societies already administered as garrisons, like China (with a tiny number of detected cases) and Cuba (with a significant number of the already ill), are responding more rapidly and peremptorily. AIDS is everyone's Trojan horse: six months before the 1988 Olympics the South Korean government announced that it would be distributing free condoms to all foreign participants. "This is a totally foreign disease, and the only way to stop its spread is to stop sexual contacts between Indians and foreigners," declared the director general of the Indian government's Council for Medical Research, thereby avowing the total defenselessness of a population nearing a billion for which there are presently *no* trained hospital staff members or treatment centers anywhere specializing in the disease. His proposal for a sexual ban, to be enforced by fines and prison terms, is no less impractical as a means of curbing sexually transmitted diseases than the more commonly made proposals for quarantine—that is, for detention. The incarceration in detention camps surrounded by barbed wire during World War I of some thirty thousand American women, prostitutes and women suspected of being prostitutes, for the avowed purpose of controlling syphilis among army recruits, caused no drop in the military's rate of infection—just as incarceration during World War II of tens of thousands of Americans of Japanese ancestry as potential traitors and spies probably did not foil a single act of espionage or sabotage. That does not mean that comparable proposals for AIDS will not be made, or will not find support, and not only by the predictable people. If the medical establishment has been on the whole a bulwark of sanity and rationality so far, refusing even to envisage programs of quarantine and detention, it may be in part because the dimensions of the crisis still seem limited and the evolution of the disease unclear.

Uncertainty about how much the disease will spread—how soon and to whom—remains at the center of public discourse about AIDS. Will it, as it spreads around the world, remain restricted, largely, to marginal populations: to the so-called risk groups and then to large sections of the urban poor? Or will it eventually become the classic pandemic affecting entire regions? Both views are in fact being held simultaneously. A wave of statements and articles affirming that AIDS threatens everybody is followed by another wave of articles asserting that it is a disease of "them," not "us." At the beginning of 1987, the U.S. Secretary of Health and Human Services predicted that the worldwide AIDS epidemic would eventually make the Black Death—the greatest epidemic ever recorded, which wiped out between a third and a half of the population of Europe—seem "pale by comparison." At the end of the year he said: "This is not a massive, widely spreading epidemic among heterosexuals as so many people fear." Even more striking than the cyclical character of public discourse about AIDS is the readiness of so many to envisage the most far-reaching of catastrophes.

Reassurances are multiplying in the United States and Western Europe that "the general population" is safe. But "the general population" may be as much a code phrase for whites as it is for heterosexuals. Everyone knows that a disproportionate number of blacks are getting AIDS, as there is a disproportionate number of blacks in the armed forces and a vastly disproportionate number in prisons. "The AIDS virus is an equal-opportunity destroyer" was the slogan of a recent fund-raising campaign by the American Foundation for AIDS Research. Punning on "equal-opportunity employer," the phrase subliminally reaffirms what it means to deny: that AIDS is an illness that in this part of the world afflicts minorities, racial and sexual. And about the staggering prediction made recently by the World Health Organization that, barring improbably rapid progress in the development of a vaccine, there will be ten to twenty times more AIDS cases in the next five years than there were in the last five, it is assumed that most of these millions will be Africans.

•

AIDS quickly became a global event—discussed not only in New York, Paris, Rio, Kinshasa but also in Helsinki, Buenos Aires, Beijing, and Singapore—when it was far from the leading cause of death in Africa, much less in the world. There are famous diseases, as there are famous countries, and these are not necessarily the ones with the biggest populations. AIDS did not become so famous just because it afflicts whites too, as some Africans bitterly assert. But it is certainly true that were AIDS only an African disease, however many millions were dying, few outside of Africa would be concerned with it. It would be one of those "natural" events, like famines, which periodically ravage poor, overpopulated countries and about which people in rich countries feel quite helpless. Because it is a world event—that is, because it affects the West—it is regarded as not just a natural disaster. It is filled with historical meaning. (Part of the self-definition of Europe and the neo-European countries is that it, the

First World, is where major calamities are history-making, transformative, while in poor, African or Asian countries they are part of a cycle, and therefore something like an aspect of nature.) Nor has AIDS become so publicized because, as some have suggested, in rich countries the illness first afflicted a group of people who were all men, almost all white, many of them educated, articulate, and knowledgeable about how to lobby and organize for public attention and resources devoted to the disease. AIDS occupies such a large part in our awareness because of what it has been taken to represent. It seems the very model of all the catastrophes privileged populations feel await them.

What biologists and public health officials predict is something far worse than can be imagined or than society (and the economy) can tolerate. No responsible official holds out the slightest hope that the African economies and health services can cope with the spread of the disease predicted for the near future, while every day one can read the direst estimates of the cost of AIDS to the country that has reported the largest number of cases, the United States. Astonishingly large sums of money are cited as the cost of providing minimum care to people who will be ill in the next few years. (This is assuming that the reassurances to "the general population" are justified, an assumption much disputed within the medical community.) Talk in the United States, and not only in the United States, is of a national emergency, "possibly our nation's survival." An editorialist at *The New York Times* intoned last year: "We all know the truth, every one of us. We live in a time of plague such as has never been visited on our nation. We can pretend it does not exist, or exists for those others, and carry on as if we do not know. . . ." And one French poster shows a giant UFO-like black mass hovering over and darkening with spidery rays most of the familiar hexagon shape of the country lying below. Above the image is written: "It depends on each of us to erase that shadow" (*Il depend de chacun de nous d'effacer cette ombre.*) And underneath: "France doesn't want to die of AIDS" (*La France ne veut pas mourir du sida*). Such token appeals for mass mobilization to confront an unprecedented menace appear, at frequent intervals, in every mass society. It is also typical of a modern society that the demand for mobilization be kept very general and the reality of the response fall well short of what seems to be demanded to meet the challenge of the nation-endangering menace. This sort of rhetoric has a life of its own: it serves some purpose if it simply keeps in circulation an ideal of unifying communal practice that is precisely contradicted by the pursuit of accumulation and isolating entertainments enjoined on the citizens of a modern mass society.

The survival of the nation, of civilized society, of the world itself is said to be at stake—claims that are a familiar part of building a case for repression. (An emergency requires "drastic measures," et cetera.)

The end-of-the-world rhetoric that AIDS has evoked does inevitably build such a case. But it also does something else. It offers a stoic, finally numbing contemplation of catastrophe. The eminent Harvard historian of science Stephen Jay Gould has declared that the AIDS pandemic may rank with nuclear weaponry "as the greatest danger of our era." But even if it kills as much as a quarter of the human race— a prospect Gould considers possible—"there will still be plenty of us left and we can start again." Scornful of the jeremiads of the moralists, a rational and humane scientist proposes the minimum consolation: an apocalypse that doesn't have any meaning. AIDS is a "natural phenomenon," not an event "with a moral meaning," Gould points out; "there is no message in its spread." Of course, it is monstrous to attribute meaning, in the sense of moral judgment, to the spread of an infectious disease. But perhaps it is only a little less monstrous to be invited to contemplate death on this horrendous scale with equanimity.

Much of the well-intentioned public discourse in our time expresses a desire to be candid about one or another of the various dangers which might be leading to all-out catastrophe. And now there is one more. To the death of oceans and lakes and forests, the unchecked growth of populations in the poor parts of the world, nuclear accidents like Chernobyl, the puncturing and depletion of the ozone layer, the perennial threat of nuclear confrontation between the superpowers or nuclear attack by one of the rogue states not under superpower control—to all these, now add AIDS. In the countdown to a millennium, a rise in apocalyptic thinking may be inevitable. Still, the amplitude of the fantasies of doom that AIDS has inspired can't be explained by the calendar alone, or even by the very real danger the illness represents. There is also the need for an apocalyptic scenario that is specific to "Western" society, and perhaps even more so to the United States. (America, as someone has said, is a nation with the soul of a church—an evangelical church prone to announcing radical endings and brand-new beginnings.) The taste for worst-case scenarios reflects the need to master fear of what is felt to be uncontrollable. It also expresses an imaginative complicity with disaster. The sense of cultural distress or failure gives rise to the desire for a clean sweep, a tabula rasa. No one wants a plague, of course. But, yes, it would be a chance to begin again. And beginning again—that is very modern, very American, too.

AIDS may be extending the propensity for becoming inured to vistas of global annihilation which the stocking and brandishing of nuclear arms has already promoted. With the inflation of apocalyptic rhetoric has come the increasing unreality of the apocalypse. A permanent modern scenario: apocalypse looms . . . and it doesn't occur. And it still looms. We seem to be in the throes of one of the modern kinds of apocalypse. There is the one that's not happening, whose outcome remains in suspense: the missiles circling the earth above our heads, with a nuclear payload that could destroy all life many times over, that haven't (so far) gone off. And there are ones that are happening, and yet seem not to have (so far) the most feared consequences—like the astronomical Third World debt, like overpopulation, like ecological blight; or that happen and then (we are told) didn't happen—like the October 1987 stock market collapse, which was a "crash," like the one in October 1929, and was not. Apocalypse is now a long-running serial: not "Apocalypse Now" but "Apocalypse From Now On." Apocalypse has become an event that is happening and not happening. It may be that some of the most feared events, like those involving the irreparable ruin of the environment, have already happened. But we don't know it yet, because the standards have changed. Or because we do not have the right indices for measuring the catastrophe. Or simply because this is a catastrophe in slow motion. (Or *feels* as if it is in slow motion, because we know about it, can anticipate it; and now have to wait for it to happen, to catch up with what we think we know.)

Modern life accustoms us to live with the intermittent awareness of monstrous, unthinkable—but, we are told, quite probable—disasters. Every major event is haunted, and not only by its representation as an image (an old doubling of reality now, which began in 1839, with the invention of the camera). Besides the photographic or electronic simulation of events, there is also the calculation of their eventual outcome. Reality has bifurcated, into the real thing and an alternative version of it, twice over. There is the event and its image. And there is the event and its projection. But as real events often seem to have no more reality for people than images, and to need the confirmation of their images, so our reaction to events in the present seeks confirmation in a mental outline, with appropriate computations, of the event in its projected, ultimate form.

Future-mindedness is as much the distinctive mental habit, and intellectual corruption, of this century as the history-mindedness that, as Nietzsche pointed out, transformed thinking in the nineteenth century. Being able to estimate how matters will evolve into the future is an inevitable byproduct of a more sophisticated (quantifiable, testable) understanding of process, social as well as scientific. The ability to project events with some accuracy into the future enlarged what power consisted of, because it was a vast new source of instructions about how to deal with the present. But in fact the look into the future, which was once tied to a vision of linear progress, has, with more knowledge at our disposal than anyone could have dreamed, turned into a vision of disaster. Every process is a prospect, and invites a prediction bolstered by statistics. Say: the number now . . . in three years, in five years, in ten years; and, of course, at the end of the century. Anything in history or nature that can be described as changing steadily can be seen as heading toward catastrophe. (Either the too little and becoming less: waning, decline, entropy. Or the too much, ever more than we can handle or absorb: uncontrollable growth.) Most of what experts pronounce about the future contributes to this new double sense of reality—beyond the doubleness to which we are already accustomed by the comprehensive duplication of everything in images. There is what is happening now. And there is what it portends: the imminent, but not yet actual, and not really graspable, disaster.

Two kinds of disaster, actually. And a gap between them, in which the imagination flounders. The difference between the epidemic we have and the pandemic that we are promised (by current statistical extrapolations) feels like the difference between the wars we have, so-called limited wars, and the unimaginably more terrible ones we could have, the latter (with all the appurtenances of science fiction) being the sort of activity people are addicted to staging for fun, as electronic games. For beyond the real epidemic with its inexorably mounting death toll (statistics are issued by national and international health organizations every week, every month) is a qualitatively different, much greater disaster which we think both will and will not take place. Nothing is changed when the most appalling estimates are revised downward, temporarily, which is an occasional feature of the display of speculative statistics disseminated by health bureaucrats and journalists. Like the demographic predictions, which are probably just as accurate, the big news is usually bad.

A proliferation of reports or projections of unreal (that is, ungraspable) doomsday eventualities tends to produce a variety of reality-denying responses. Thus, in most discussions of nuclear warfare, being rational (the self-description of experts) means not acknowledging the human reality, while taking in emotionally even a small part of what is at stake for human beings (the province of those who regard themselves as the menaced) means insisting on unrealistic demands for the rapid dismantling of the peril. This split of public attitude, into the inhuman and the all-too-human, is much less stark with AIDS. Experts denounce the stereotypes attached to people with AIDS and to the continent where it is presumed to have originated, emphasizing that the disease belongs to much wider populations than the groups initially at risk, and to the whole world, not just to Africa.* For while AIDS has turned out, not surprisingly,

* "AIDS cannot be stopped in any country unless it is stopped in all countries," declared the retiring head of the World Health Organization in Geneva, Dr. Halfdan Mahler, at the Fourth International Conference on AIDS (Stockholm, June 1988), where the global character of the AIDS crisis was a leading theme. "This epidemic is worldwide and is sparing no continent," said Dr. Willy Rozenbaum, a French AIDS specialist. "It cannot be mastered in the West unless it is overcome everywhere." In contrast to the rhetoric of global responsibility, a specialty of the international conferences, is the view, increasingly heard, in which AIDS is regarded as a kind of Darwinian test of a society's aptitude for survival, which may require writing off those countries that can't defend themselves. A German AIDS specialist, Dr. Eike Brigitte Helm, has declared that it "can already be seen that in a number of parts of the world AIDS will drastically change the population structure. Particularly in Africa and Latin America. A society that is not able, somehow or other, to prevent the spread of AIDS has very poor prospects for the future."

to be one of the most meaning-laden of diseases, along with leprosy and syphilis, clearly there are checks on the impulse to stigmatize people with the disease. The way in which the illness is such a perfect repository for people's most general fears about the future to some extent renders irrelevant the predictable efforts to pin the disease on a deviant group or a dark continent.

Like the effects of industrial pollution and the new system of global financial markets, the AIDS crisis is evidence of a world in which nothing important is regional, local, limited; in which everything that can circulate does, and every problem is, or is destined to become, worldwide. Goods circulate (including images and sounds and documents, which circulate fastest of all, electronically). Garbage circulates: the poisonous industrial wastes of St. Etienne, Hannover, Mestre, and Bristol are being dumped in the coastal towns of West Africa. People circulate, in greater numbers than ever. And diseases. From the untrammeled intercontinental air travel for pleasure and business of the privileged to the unprecedented migrations of the underprivileged from villages to cities and, legally and illegally, from country to country— all this physical mobility and interconnectedness (with its consequent dissolving of old taboos, social and sexual) is as vital to the maximum functioning of the advanced, or world, capitalist economy as is the easy transmissibility of goods and images and financial instruments. But now that heightened, modern interconnectedness in space, which is not only personal but social, structural, is the bearer of a health menace sometimes described as a threat to the species itself; and the fear of AIDS is of a piece with attention to other unfolding disasters that are the byproduct of advanced society, particularly those illustrating the degradation of the environment on a world scale. AIDS is one of the dystopian harbingers of the global village, that future which is already here and always before us, which no one knows how to refuse.

•

That even an apocalypse can be made to seem part of the ordinary horizon of expectation constitutes an unparalleled violence that is being done to our sense of reality, to our humanity. But it is highly desirable for a specific dreaded illness to come to seem ordinary. Even the disease most fraught with meaning can become just an illness. It has happened with leprosy, though some ten million people in the world, easy to ignore since almost all live in Africa and the Indian subcontinent, have what is now called, as part of its wholesome dedramatization, Hansen's disease (after the Norwegian physician who, over a century ago, discovered the bacillus). It is bound to happen with AIDS, when the illness is much better understood and, above all, treatable. For the time being, much in the way of individual experience and social policy depends on the struggle for rhetorical ownership of the illness: how it is possessed, assimilated in argument and in cliché. The age-old, seemingly inexorable process whereby diseases acquire meanings (by coming to stand for the deepest fears) and inflict stigma is always worth challenging, and it does seem to have more limited credibility in the modern world, among people willing to be modern—the process is under surveillance now. With this illness, one that elicits so much guilt and shame, the effort to detach it from these meanings, these metaphors, seems particularly liberating, even consoling. But the metaphors cannot be distanced just by abstaining from them. They have to be exposed, criticized, belabored, used up.

Not all metaphors applied to illnesses and their treatment are equally unsavory and distorting. The one I am most eager to see retired—more than ever since the emergence of AIDS—is the military metaphor. Its converse, the medical model of the public weal, is probably more dangerous and far-reaching in its consequences, since it not only provides a persuasive justification for authoritarian rule but implicitly suggests the necessity of state-sponsored repression and violence (the equivalent of surgical removal or chemical control of the offending or "unhealthy" parts of the body politic). But the effect of the military imagery on thinking about sickness and health is far from inconsequential. It overmobilizes, it overdescribes, and it powerfully contributes to the excommunicating and stigmatizing of the ill.

No, it is not desirable for medicine, any more than

for war, to be "total." Neither is the crisis created by AIDS a "total" anything. We are not being invaded. The body is not a battlefield. The ill are neither unavoidable casualties nor the enemy. We—medicine, society—are not authorized to fight back by any means whatever. . . . About that metaphor, the military one, I would say, if I may paraphrase Lucretius: Give it back to the war-makers.